and Death; and we are subdued and thrilled with a sense of something as far beyond our tiny tasks and griefs as the awakening of nature is beyond our waking from the slumbers of the night.

> "On move the resurrection hours,
> The Easter heralds throng—
> Till sudden bursts the miracle
> Of blossom and of song!"

THE END

THE MEN'S HOUSE

Books by the Same Author

THE BUILDERS

SHORT TALKS ON MASONRY

RELIGION OF MASONRY
(Out of print)

MODERN MASONRY
(Contained in LITTLE MASONIC LIBRARY)

BROTHERS AND SISTERS
(Incorporated in SHORT TALKS ON MASONRY)

RIVERS OF YEARS
(Autobiography—Out of print)

THE MEN'S HOUSE
Masonic Papers and Addresses

by

Joseph Fort Newton, Litt.D.

*"The Brotherhood of Man begins with
the Manhood of the Brother."*
Wm. N. Ponton

Macoy Publishing & Masonic Supply Co., Inc.
Richmond, Virginia

Copyright, 1923
Masonic Service Association of the United States

Copyright, 1969, 1990
Macoy Publishing & Masonic Supply Co., Inc.
Richmond, Virginia

ISBN-0-88053-037-5

Printed in the United States of America

TO
HARRY LEROY HAYWOOD
Editor of *The Builder*
A FELLOW-WORKMAN
ON THE TEMPLE

A TRIBUTE TO
JOSEPH FORT NEWTON
by Allen E. Roberts

NO MAN could turn prose into poetry more effectively than Joseph Fort Newton, D.D. No man has had his beautiful phrases pirated more often.

No man loved his fellowman more deeply. No Freemason loved the philosophy and principles of the Craft more earnestly than did Joseph Fort Newton. He says so on the first page of this book: "Freemasonry appeals to me, first, by its fellowship; and next to the home and the House of God, it is the most blessed influence in my life." These were not empty words for Newton.

Why? Why did a man who had reached the pinnacle in religious and other circles find Freemasonry so intriguing? How did he discover the Craft in the first place? Some of the answers will be found in his autobiography *River of Years:*

> My father had been a soldier in the Southern army, hardly more than a boy, afraid the war would soon be over before he got into it. Afterward he was afraid it would never be over. He was made a Mason in a military Lodge, and wore a red string in the lapel of his coat. Taken prisoner at Arkansas Post, he was carried up the Mississippi River to Rock Island, Illinois. The Northern climate was severe on Southern men, as the records of the War Deparment reveal.

> My father became ill, desperately ill, and made himself known as a Mason to an officer of the prison. The officer took him to his own home and nursed him back to life. When the war ended, he loaned Father money to pay his way back to his Texas home, and gave him a pearl-handled pistol to protect himself.
>
> They remained close friends and my father tried, later, to induce his officer-friend to come to Texas and be his partner at law.
>
> This experience of my father, when I learned about it, had a very great influence upon my life, as will appear later; the fact that such a fraternity of men could exist, mitigating the harshness of war, and remain unbroken when states and churches were torn in two, became a wonder; and it is not strange that I tried for years to repay my debt to it.

Unlike most famous men who actually owe more than they will admit to the teachings of Freemasonry, Newton never hesitated to proclaim his loyalty to the Craft.

Joseph Newton was born July 21, 1876. He was almost seven years old when his father, Lee, died. Joseph recalled the Masonic funeral service conducted by the lodge over which his father had once presided as Master. And he appreciated the many Masons who "came to ask Mother if they could help her in any way."

Joseph was disturbed by schisms. He felt it was absurd to have two Methodist churches, one North and one South, in his small town. The elders and the children worked and played together, "but when they went to worship, each went his own way...In other words, religion, which ought to have united the community, divided it."

Joseph Newton, to his regret, never learned to dance. It was prohibited by his church. He did become the first "boy in town to learn to throw a ball that curved to the left, which made a right-handed batter look foolish fanning the air." He would become a life-long fan of the American sport called "baseball."

Early in his youth Newton obtained a copy of Leo Tolstoy's *War and Peace.* About it he had this to say:

> It would be impossible for me to describe the impression made upon me by that stupendous story, perhaps the greatest novel ever written. Mother, of course, got more out of it than I did—its vast canvas, its throng of characters, with jaw-breaking names, confused me somewhat. But one scene stuck in my mind and stayed, the talk of the old Freemason with Pierre when the nobleman said he did not believe in God:
>
> "You do not know Him, Sir, and that is why you are unhappy. Of Whom were we speaking? Whom dost thou deny? Who invented Him, if He were not? How came there within thee the conception that there is such an incomprehensible Being?...Yes, God exists, but to know Him is hard. It is not attained by reason, but by life."
>
> Thus, to Tolstoi [1] I owe an insight which has guided me through the years—that religion would not exist if the Object of religion did not exist; its Object which is also its origin. There would be nothing to suggest it, nothing to sustain it. For that reason, I have never tried to prove God—what kind of a God could my little mind prove? How would I go about it."

When Newton was fourteen his maternal grandfather Battle died. Joseph was deeply moved and his mother was devastated. Not knowing what to do, he walked into the woodland close by. At the top of a hill he sat and stared at the creek below. "Suddenly all my trouble, all my fear, left me," he wrote. Life itself seemed to speak to my spirit. God became very near, very real, not awful but gentle as a Friend; Jesus infinitely enlarged in every way—but something more. My whole being was aware of Him, with an intense stillness."

A short time later a new teacher by the name of Roberts came to town. Among the important things he taught his students was how to think on their feet. He made them speak extemporaneously—and on both sides of any subject! Newton credits him with his later ability to speak and to approach all subjects with an open mind, to reach truth.

Learning that Newton planned on entering the ministry, Roberts told him: "If a preacher cannot remember his own sermon long enough to preach it, nobody will remember it long after he does preach it."

Which ministry to enter posed a problem for Newton. He discussed his doubts with his mother. She wisely told him: Listen only to Jesus. Accept what He says about God, what He shows God to be in His life, nothing else, nothing less; test everything by Him—forget the rest."

Newton entered the Baptist ministry. The ordination took place in the Methodist church, because it was the largest church in town. It was crowded.

He later said he was ordained at the age of nineteen. This must be an error. He was only eighteen when he went to the seminary, and that was after serving his first church. He doesn't mention how long he served.

His first church was at Rose Hill in Texas. At this time one Baptist church couldn't commune with any other. And the various religious factions didn't mix. He did not belive in the Baptist theology. "To me," he wrote, "the dogma of eternal hell was abhorrent; it meant the worship of a defeated God...the Protestant hell surging on in omnipotent fury forever is the most frightful dogma every promulgated in times not actually barbaric." He immediately "began to build bridges and break down barriers," something he would do throughout his life.

His ministry was a success, but in 1894 he went off to the Southern Baptist Theological Seminary at Louisville, Kentucky. He was greeted by an actual earthquake! While attending this seminary he visited the local Jewish synagogue. For this he was accused of heresy! He also served as "associate chaplain of a great gray prison across the river, in Indiana."

Newton claimed: "The fact remains that the things which did most for my development, and lived longest in my heart, were the books I read outside the field of theology." But a book on theology that "talked in terms of salvation, not salvage," did influence his thinking for many years.

Fate sent him to Sanders, Kentucky, to take over the pulpit of a friend for a month. There he met his "Dream Girl," the organ player, whom he would call "Lady Brown-eyes." On June 14, 1900, she, Virginia Mai Deatherage, and Newton were married in the Fifth Avenue Hotel in Louisville, Kentucky. They left immediately for St. Louis, Missouri. There he had taken over the Non-Sectarian Church of St. Louis.

"More and more it becomes clear that I needed to take further courses of study," wrote Newton. "I wanted to make new contacts and explore new fields." So he left for Boston, Massachusetts. Among the many influential people he met was Frank B. Sanborn, who later started Newton on his long study of Abraham Lincoln. He preached "in many kinds of churches, feeling at home in each." He later wrote: "The men I met in New England and talked with—or rather listened to—united the two most precious things in life, the spiritual quality and the vital mind."

In 1903 he left for Dixon, Illinois, and with the backing of many formed a "People's Church."

Newton didn't think too highly of the politicians in Dixon. He believed they were taking a middle road between the traffickers in liguor and the "nice people." About this time Billy Sunday was invited to hold a revival in the town. He came. He prayed for all the ministers in town—except Newton! Newton wrote: "Sunday preached the most ghastly caricature of religion—to say nothing of the Gospel of Jesus—which has ever been my sadness to hear."

In Friendship Lodge No. 7, Dixon, Illinois, at the age of 21, Newton was made a Master Mason. Of this experience he wrote: "There, to my amazement, I saw men of all churches—except one, and there was no reason in Masonry why that one church could not be represented—gathered about an open Bible. In their churches they could not agree about the teachings of the Bible; in the Lodge they could not disagree, because each one was allowed to interpret it in the way his heart loved best, and asked to allow others the same right; a secret almost too simple to be found out."

Actors were frowned upon. Preachers ignored them. The parents of a child wanted it christened. This was never done in a Baptist church, so when Newton was approached he didn't know what to do. But he said he'd do it. He couldn't find anything suitable anywhere. He wrote his own ritual, then christened the child.

"To my distress," he wrote, "the story got into the papers." A short time later he was appointed a chaplain of the Actor's Church Alliance. This brought him into contact with members of the acting profession all over the world.

He wrote the biograpy titled *David Swing, Poet-Preacher*. As a consequence he was invited to take over the Liberal Christian Church in Cedar Rapids, Iowa. It would become better known as "The Little Brick Church." It was there that he became more fully acquainted with Freemasonry. The magnificent Masonic library in Cedar Rapids beckoned him. His books would later find a safe repository there.

In his autobiography Newton said: "Even to this day, though I have wondered afar to London, and great cities in our own land, Cedar Rapids still seems more like home to me than any place on earth."

It was in Cedar Rapids that Newton worked on this book *Lincoln & Herndon* which was published in 1910. It was here that the Grand Master requested Newton to write a book telling Masons the story and meaning of Freemasonry. The result was *The Builders, A Story and Study of Freemasonry*. It was published in England and translated and published in Dutch, Swedish, Spanish, Sanskrit and just recently (1989) Finnish. It has become perhaps the most widely read Masonic book ever printed.

It was also in Cedar Rapids that Newton helped George Schoonover form the National Masonic Research Society. Newton became the first editor of its excellent periodical, *The Builder*. He remained its editor after he was called to be the minister of City Temple in London, England, in 1915. His adventures there throughout the war could fill a volume of its own.

To the Church of the Divine Paternity in New York City Newton transferred at war's end. He wasn't happy there. He found the stress and tension unhealthy. He was attempting to do too much: speeches, preaching everywhere; lectures in colleges from Maine to Mississippi, plus the University of Iowa on many occasions, editing publications such as *Best Sermons* and *The Master Mason* for The Masonic Service Association.

He doesn't mention the work he was doing in an attempt to save The Masonic Service Association from extinction. This servant of the Craft was under attack by individuals who hadn't learned to practice without their lodges the lessons taught within them. He, along with Carl H. Claudy, did save it, but barely.

Newton, the independent minister, the man of God who found the prevailing theology in conflict with the will of the Supreme Being, was asked to affiliate with the Episcopal Church! Bishop Garland and Newton discussed their views on the need for "only one Church of Christ on earth." They found they had much in common, including the fact that they were Brother Masons.

Newton became an Episcopalian priest! From 1938 he found the peace he had been seeking as Rector of the Church of St. Luke and the Epiphany in

Philadelphia which he served until January 24, 1950, when he suffered a heart attack and died. He had been active until the end. On the Sunday before, he preached his final sermon in his church.

The full story of Joseph Fort Newton reads like a romance. As with the books he wrote for the edification and enjoyment of Freemasons, the story of his life is difficult to condense in this short tribute.

A phrase Newton used to describe an attack on a minister remained with me since I read it many years ago. "He told the truth, but not the whole truth, and a half-truth was equal to a lie!"

The search for the whole truth was a philosophy Newton followed throughout his career as a minister of God and a Freemason.

INTRODUCTION TO THE MACOY EDITION

TO THE FREEMASON, be he only beginning his work in the quarries of the Craft, or a laborer of many years standing, these inspiring writings and addresses from one of the Craft's most eloquent authors, will bring joy and meaning. Their patriotic and spiritual appeal will be welcomed by the non-Mason as well and bring a new understanding and help in meeting the everyday problems facing human society yesterday, today, and tomorrow.

Perhaps most quoted of all Dr. Newton's messages is "When is a man a Mason?" contained in the third chapter of this book. In these 38 lines, Dr. Newton gives thought for a life's time study.

THE PUBLISHER

1969

IN THE QUARRY

For years I have had repeated requests from many Brethren, both in England and in America, asking me to gather various papers and addresses on Masonic themes into a form more convenient and accessible. The present selection is not complete, but it may serve the purpose desired, and perhaps give cumulative effect to words spoken at different times and places, at home and abroad, in the service of our great and gentle Craft.

Inevitably, in a series of addresses covering ten years or more, there will be some repetition of idea, if not of phrase; but it has seemed best to let them stand as they were written, the more because the great truths need to be emphasized with many variations of insight and accent. During the period covered by these papers my little book, *The Builders*, was written, and is still busy at its work in many lands and four or five languages; and its readers will find much that is familiar in these pages.

Freemasonry appeals to me, first, by its fellowship; and next to the home and the House of God, it is the most blessed influence in my life. Its simple and profound faith, its wise and practical philosophy—uniting the wisdom of love with the love of wisdom—illumine my mind, as its genius of fraternity warms my heart. But still more Masonry appeals to me as an agency for the organization of moral faith, practical brotherhood, and social idealism, the worth and power of which we have not yet realized.

Most of the words of this book were spoken while the Great War and the Little Peace were sweeping over us, leaving disaster, desolation, and disillusionment in their wake. They have gone, those years, dark, dreadful, and confused; but, by the mercy of God, the ideals set forth in these pages still glow and abide in the heart of the speaker; and he makes bold once more to commend them to his fellow-workmen on the Temple. In a day when the brotherhood of the world is broken, our ancient and noble Craft has an opportunity, the like of which it has never known before, to use its influence and power to spread that fraternal righteousness without which the future will be as dark as the past.

For the rest, my gratitude is due to Brother H. L. Haywood, editor of *The Builder*, who has kindly allowed me to use certain papers which appeared in its pages when I had the honor of being its first editor. Also to Brother Douglas Martin, of the Detroit *Masonic News*, for the use of a number of articles which appeared in his bright and forward-looking journal; as well as for personal kindnesses which make a rosary in my memory. To all my Brethren everywhere, the very thought of whom is like music, I send greeting, blessing, and abounding goodwill.

J.F.N.

Church of the Divine Paternity,
New York City

THE TRESTLE BOARD

CHAPTER	PAGE

PART ONE: *Principles*

I	The Men's House	1
II	The Mission of Masonry	13
III	The Ministry of Masonry	36
IV	The Geometry of God	57
V	The Bible in Masonry	68
VI	Religion and Masonry	74
VII	The Builders	83

PART TWO: *Practice*

VIII	Practical Brotherhood	85
IX	The Doctrine of the Balance	97
X	The Master	107
XI	Knights of a New Crusade	112
XII	Masonry in American History	121
XIII	The Cornerstone of the Future	133
XIV	The Flag of Peace	143

PART THREE: *Personalities*

XV	The Spirit of Robert Burns	145
XVI	"Father" Taylor	153
XVII	Edwin Markham	167
XVIII	Albert Pike	178
XIX	Rudyard Kipling	198

PART FOUR: *Prophecy*

Chapter		Page
XX	The Patriarchs	207
XXI	"Solemn Strikes the Funeral Chime"	221
XXII	Those Gone Before	229
XXIII	The Day of Eternal Hope	233

PART ONE: *Principles*

Chapter I

THE MEN'S HOUSE

I

History, in the great conception of it, reveals a romance more fantastic than all fiction. The first words of the Bible are still true, "In the beginning God"; but to-day science writes a commentary on those words which staggers the imagination. Against "the old, dark, backward abysm of time"—a deep no reckoning can fathom—it sees the dawn of an amazing, bewildering Day, to which all geological cycles led up, and for which the world through untold ages had been preparing and cooling: a day of days when man first stood upon the earth, helpless and innocent, with a new light in his mind and a strange longing in his heart.

> "A fire-mist and a planet,
>   A crystal and a cell,
> A jelly-fish and a saurian,
>   And caves where the cave-men dwell;

> Then a sense of law and beauty,
>   And a face turned from the clod—
> Some call it evolution,
>   And others call it God."

God-illumined, but not yet God-conquered—the history of the race is the story of the self-discovery of man, which is also a revelation of God. Frail and fleeting in the midst of brute forces, he was yet different from the brute, having a faculty divine, a power to master and harness the forces of nature. Wasps, bees, and birds do now what they did at first; they do not create. Man alone responded to the Creative Spirit and moved into ever larger life, where faith supports, hope leads on, and love consecrates. As the ice age passed, he followed up its retreat, his home a cave with rude stone tools lying on the floor. Families, in the second generation, became tribes, and tribes merged into nations. By such unions Brotherhood took shape, precariously at the mercy of feuds and wars. Yet, through all primitive savageries, God kept alive the principle of Brotherhood; at once a necessity and a prophecy—a law written in the nature of man and the will of the Eternal. The tragedy of trying to solve the making of a man or a nation, in defiance of the Principles of Brotherhood, is written in letters of blood and fire, ancient and modern.

> "There is an unseen cord that binds
> The whole wide world together;
> Through every human life it winds,
> This one mysterious tether.
> There are no separate lives; the chain,
> Too subtle for our seeing,
> Unites us all upon the plane
> Of universal being."

II

In primitive society there were four institutions, equally Divine, equally sacred, all tokens of the solidarity of aspiration and obligation, of need and destiny, which binds humanity together. There was, first of all, and most fundamental, the Home—the corner stone of society and civilization, which satisfies more human needs than any other fellowship. It was crude, as all things were in the morning of time, yet it had in it the prophecy of that enshrinement of beauty and tenderness into which we were born, the memory of which hallows us still. The basic fact in the human story is the family as the unit of values, marking the life of man off from anything known or looked for in the animal world. To contrast its early simplicity with the religious and social refinement of to-day is to fill the word Progress with an unimagined meaning.

There was the Temple of Prayer—not a temple

at first, but only a rough altar of uncut stone—uplifted by the same instinct for the Eternal which built the great cathedrals. Its rites were rude, often grotesque and horrible—its smoke of sacrifice ascending in a cloud of fear—yet in that darkness there was a gleam of "the light that never was on sea or land," by which we are guided through the labyrinth of the world. There was the State, beginning in patriarchal rule, merging thence into the tribe and the nation, and at last into huge empires which met in the clash of conflict. The State, too, was imperfect—as it still is—but it had in it the rudiments and foregleams of our patriotic devotion to our Republic.

But there was another institution, quite as old as the other three, equally sacred and hardly less important, to which we are more indebted than we realize. It was called the Men's House, a secret lodge in which every young man, when he came to maturity, was initiated into the law, legend, and tradition of his people. Recent research has brought to light this long hidden institution, showing that it was really the center of early tribal life, the council chamber, the guest house, the place of meeting for men, where laws were made and courts were held, and where the trophies of war were treasured.[1] Indeed, early

[1] For a scientific study of the Men's House, see "Primitive Secret Societies," by Prof. Hutton Webster, especially chapters 1-4 and 10-11.

human society—most of it, at least, so far as the men were concerned—was a secret society; and unless we keep this fact in mind we can hardly understand it at all. It is a key to the interpretation of primitive social life, without which many things remain cryptic and shadowy.

It is not easy to exaggerate the importance of these secret lodges in the formative period of society in promoting that sense of kinship, sanctity, and loyalty which lies at the roots of law, order and religion. Methods of initiation differed in different times and places, but they had, nevertheless, a certain likeness, as they had always the same purpose. Ordeals, often frightful, were required—exposing the initiate not only to physical danger, but to the perils of unseen spirits—as tests to prove youth worthy, by reason of valor and virtue, to be entrusted with the secret lore of the tribe. The ceremonies included vows of chastity, of courage, of secrecy and loyalty, and, almost always, a drama representing the advent of the novice into his new life of privilege and responsibility. Moreover, the new life to which he awoke after his "initiation into manhood," for such it truly was, included a new name, a new language of signs, grips and tokens, whereby to make himself known to his fellows in the dark as well as in the light. If a youth failed to endure the tests required, and proved himself to be a coward or a weakling, he became the scorn of every man of the tribe.

To-day, as never before, we understand the place of the secret society, or lodge, in the development of civilization, and that the Men's House, along with the home and the temple, is one of the oldest institutions of man. When the tribe ceased to be the unit of society, giving way to the nation, the House of the Hidden Place, as it was called, became at once a school and a temple, preserving and transmitting the truths of religion, the rudiments of science, and the laws of art, all of which were universally held as sacred secrets to be known only by the initiated. By a certain instinct men felt that everything must not be told to everybody, but that men should approve themselves worthy to receive truths which had cost so much; and that instinct was wise. Even the gentle Teacher of Galilee would not cast His pearls before swine, but taught in parables, cryptic and dim.

Hence the great ancient Orders called the Mysteries, which ruled the world for ages before our era; and he who would estimate the spiritual possessions of humanity must take account of their influence and power. The Mysteries of Isis in Egypt, of Elusicina in Greece, of the Mithra in Rome, swayed mankind, using every device of art to teach the truths of faith and the principles of righteousness—and, especially, to satisfy the haunting hunger for salvation. These orders continued the tradition and ministry of the Men's House, and at their altars the greatest men of antiquity—Moses, Pythagoras, Plato, Plutarch, to name no others—received initiation. Their temples were shrines of art, schools of philosophy, and sanctuaries of religion, and from them, as time passed, the arts spread out, fanwise, along the avenues of culture.

III

History is no older than architecture. Man did not become a civilized being until he had learned to build a settled habitation, a Home, a Temple, a Memorial for his dead. So, and naturally so, the tradition of the Men's House became associated with the art of building, using the laws and tools of the builder as emblems of the truths of faith and morality. Long before our era an order of builders, known as the Dionysian Artificers, were working in Asia Minor, erecting temples, theaters, palaces—a secret order whose ceremonies perpetuated the ancient drama of the Mysteries—and they were almost certainly the builders of the Temple of Solomon on Mount Moriah. Thence we trace them westward into Rome, where they were identified with the Roman College of Architects, whose emblems have come down to us.

When Rome fell the Order of the Builders took refuge on a fortified island in Lake Como, in northern Italy, where they preserved their traditions and their art. From them descended the great fraternity of the Comacine Masters—the Cathedral Builders—whom we follow through the Middle Ages, and who early became known as Freemasons—free, because they were exempt from many restraints, and, unlike Guild Masons, were at liberty to travel where their work called them. They were great artists, commanding the service of the finest intellects of the age, yet so bound together into a fraternity that, as Hallam said, no cathedral can be traced to any one artist. The cathedrals were not the work of individual artists, but the creation of a community of artists, who united a spirit of fraternity with the sense of the sanctity of art; and so they labored until the decline of Gothic architecture and the end of the cathedral-building period.

As early as 1600, if not earlier, scholars and students of mysticism began to ask to be accepted as members of the lodges of Freemasons, the better to study their symbolism and teaching—as, for example, Ashmole, who founded the museum which bears his name at Oxford.

THE MEN'S HOUSE

These men, though not practical architects, were accepted as members of the order; hence Free and *Accepted* Masons. When the work of practical architecture became so changed as no longer to require the service of a fraternal order, the Freemasons ceased to be builders of temples of brick and stone, but retained their organization and tradition—builders no less than before, but using their tools and laws and symbols of the truths and principles with which they sought to build a Temple of Righteousness and Friendship upon earth. This newer Masonry, as it has been called, took its present form with the founding of the Grand Lodge of England, in 1717, from which it has spread over the civilized world. Forming one great society of devout and free men, it toils in every land in behalf of Freedom, Friendship and Fraternity, seeking to strengthen the social and moral sentiment which gives to law its authority and to religion its opportunity.

IV

Such is the basis and background of our gentle Craft of Freemasonry. It perpetuates in modern life the purpose of the Men's House of primitive society, and the noble tradition of the Builders. No doubt it was the antiquity and necessity of the idea of initiation that our Masonic fathers had in mind when they said that Masonry began with the beginning of history; and they were not so far wrong as certain clever folk think they were. It is rightly described in one of its old documents as "an ancient and honorable institution, as having subsisted from time immemorial; and honorable it must be acknowledged to be, as by natural tendency it conduces to make those so who are obedient to its precepts." It is not an accident of human association, nor an invention of occultists, but a fraternity rooted in the nature and need of humanity; an order of men initiated, sworn and trained to uphold all the redeeming ideals of society, and to make righteousness and the will of God prevail.

Masonry is not a political society; its ancient Constitutions forbid the discussion of political issues in its Lodges, "as what never yet conduced to the welfare of the Lodge, nor never will." It is not a Church, nor the enemy of any church of any name, but a Fellowship seeking to bring men of every faith together the better to teach them to honor and love one another; its secret the Open Secret of the world for such as have eyes to see and minds to think. In a Lodge of Masons in London, during the Great War, I saw men of all the great religions of the world, and nearly every sect of Christendom—Protestant and Catholic alike—kneel together at one

Altar, lifting up hands in prayer to one God and Father of all! Together we learned the meaning of that love without which, as St. Paul said, the most perfect theology is nothing. Nay, more; we learned that down below race, rank and creed there is only one heart in all the world, and that love is the way to it. No one can estimate the worth of such a Fraternity, much less measure its power—its unguessed, undreamed-of possibilities—for the organization and expression of that practical brotherliness in which the race will find its true destiny.

The ideal of Masonry is one with that vision of the Kingdom of Heaven which Jesus exhausted the resources of His incomparable speech —fresh as the dew and bright with color—to make real and vivid to man. Only, in Freemasonry it is set forth under the imagery of architecture: the vision of a living Temple— noble, stately, sheltering the holy things of humanity—slowly rising in the midst of the ages; a Temple building and built upon, each workman not only a builder, but himself a living stone, foursquare and finely wrought, to be built into the whole; each generation of builders adding an arch, a pillar, or a spire, as the old gray cathedrals were uplifted, strong and piteous, matching the masonry of the mountains in their grandeur; each race of Masons building upon the foundations of their vanished comrades. In height, in depth, in breadth and beauty it is the noblest vision that has dawned upon our groping human sight, flashing before even the dullest mind a vision of something immortal, something worthy of love and loyalty, something in which our fleeting life reveals its prophecy—a sequence of aim and obligation, of communal enterprise and co-operative fellowship, which annuls the ephemeral and unveils the eternal in time.

Chapter II

THE MISSION OF MASONRY [1]

To-day we have erected a bronze tablet marking the site of the first lodge of Masons in the territory of Iowa. Such a memorial of our fathers, the pioneers, is in accord with the fitness of things. It bespeaks a sense of history, a vision of the past out of which the present has come to flower, and from whose wise and prophetic sowing the fruit of the future will grow. We honor ourselves by thus recalling the men of other days, but we also lay upon ourselves the obligation to labor, as they labored, with forward-looking thoughts, while establishing more firmly the work of their hands. Others have labored; we have entered into their labors, and it behooves us to continue that sacred history.

Those sturdy men who set up the altar of Masonry on the frontier of this commonwealth were prophetic souls. They were men of faith who builded better than they knew, as men of faith always do. They believed in the future, in the growth of large things from small beginnings,

[1] Address before the Grand Lodge of Iowa at its 69th Annual Communication, Burlington, Iowa, June 13, 1912, Grand Master Block presiding.

and in the principles of Masonry as the true foundation of society and the fortress of a free state. They knew that the Masonic lodge is a silent partner of the home, the church, and the school house, toiling in behalf of law and order, without which neither industry nor art can flourish, and that its benign influence would help to build this commonwealth in strength, wisdom, and beauty. Therefore they erected their altar and kindled its flame; and having wrought in faithfulness, they died in faith, obeying the injunction of that master poet who said:

> "Keep the young generations in hail,
> Bequeath to them no tumbled house!"

Time has more than fulfilled their dream; the facts have outrun their faith. If men see, after death, what passes on this earth, what a picture now lies spread out for their rejoicing vision. They behold not only our lakes, hills, and rolling prairies, our rivers running to the sea, our cities shining in the sunlight, trains moving to and fro like shuttles in a loom, park-like farms dotted with homes, school houses and children at play, temples of prayer and the sleeping places of the dead; but also the march of ideas, the growth and flowering of principles, the unfolding of truths, the increase of liberty, justice, and fraternity among men, and the mystic ties of memory uniting the present in which we toil with the past in which they labored and fell asleep. Their greatest happiness must consist in seeing their good influences widening out from year to year, as rivulets widen into rivers, and shaping the current of history, as our influence, for weal or woe, will help to shape the times to come.

Under the spell of such a vision we may well pause, look before and after, and ask ourselves the meaning of this fraternity and its mission among men. One of the most impressive and touching things in human history is that certain ideal interests have been set apart as especially venerated among all peoples. Guilds have arisen to cultivate the interests embodied in art, science, philosophy, fraternity, and religion, to train men in their service, to bring their power to bear upon the common life of mortals and send through that common life the glory of the ideal, as the sun shoots its transfiguring rays through the great dull cloud, evoking beauty from the brown earth. Such is Masonry, which unites all these high interests and brings to their service a vast, world-wide fraternity of free men, built upon a basis of spiritual faith, whose mission it is to make men friends, to refine and exalt their lives, to turn them from the semblance of life to homage for truth, righteousness, and character. Forming one great society over the whole globe, it upholds every noble and redeeming ideal of humanity, making all good things better by its presence, like a meadow that rests on a subterranean stream. He who would reckon the spiritual possessions of our race must take account of the genius of Masonry and its ministry to the highest life of man.

The very existence of such a great historic fellowship in the quest and service of the ideal is a fact eloquent beyond all words. It is like some lofty mountain uplifted in the midst of the years, at whose feet the generations come and go, whose air sweetens the world, and whose peak assembles the vagrant clouds and invokes showers of refreshing. Apparitions of a day, what is our puny warfare against ignorance and evil compared with the warfare which this venerable order has been waging against them for centuries, and will wage after we are gone? More than an institution, more than a tradition, more than a society, Masonry is one of the forms of the Divine life upon earth. No one may ever hope to describe a spirit so benign and beautiful, an influence so quiet, so unresting, so persistent, and so gracious. That task belongs of right to the genius of poetry and song, by whose magic those elusive and impalpable realities which hallow the world find embodiment and voice. All that one can do is to state the faith of Masonry, its philosophy, the basis of its demand for freedom, and its plea for universal friendship.

I

On the threshold of the Masonic lodge every man, whether prince or peasant, is asked to confess his faith in God the Father Almighty, the Architect and Master-builder of the world. That is not a mere form of words. To be indifferent to God is to be indifferent to the greatest of all realities, that upon which the aspiration of humanity rests for its uprising passion and desire. No institution that is dumb concerning the ultimate meaning and character of this universe can last. It is a house built upon the sand, doomed to fall when the winds blow and the floods beat upon it. No human brotherhood that has not its foundation in a Divine Fatherhood can long endure. It is a rope of sand, weak as water, and its fine sentiment quickly evaporates. Life leads, if we follow its meanings and move in the drift of its deeper conclusions, to one God as the ground of the world, and upon that ground Masonry lays its cornerstone. Therefore, it endures, and the gates of hell shall not prevail against it.

That reverent and enlightened faith from which, as from a never-failing spring, flow heroic devotedness, moral self-respect, authentic sentiments of fraternity, inflexible fidelity and effectual consolations, honor in life and hope in death, this great order has in all times religiously preserved. Ardently and perseveringly it has propagated it through the centuries, and in our age more zealously than ever. Scarcely a Masonic discourse is pronounced, or a Masonic lesson read, by the highest officer or the humblest lecturer, that does not earnestly teach two extremely simple and profound principles—love of God and love of our fellow man. That is the one true religion, and it is the very spirit of Masonry, its light and power, its basis and apex. Upon that faith it rests; in that faith it lives; and by that faith it will conquer, putting the doubts and bigotries of men to shame with its simple insight, and the dignity of its golden voice.

Of no one age, Masonry belongs to all time; of no one religion, it finds great truths in all. Indeed, it holds that truth which is common to all elevating and benign religions, and is the basis of each; that faith which underlies all sects and over-arches all creeds, the sky above and the river bed below the flow of mortal years. It is not a religion, still less a cult, but it is a worship in which all good men may unite, that each may share the faith of all. It does not undertake to explain or dogmatically to settle those great mysteries which out-top human knowledge. Beyond the facts of faith it does not go. With the subtleties of speculation concerning these truths, and the unworldly envies growing out of them, it has not to do. There divisions begin, and Masonry was not made to divide men, but to unite them. It asks not for tolerance, but for fraternity, leaving each man free to think his own thought and fashion his own system of ultimate truth. Therefore, all through the ages it has been, and is today, a meeting place of differing minds and a prophecy of the final union of all reverent and devout souls.

In the olden time one man framed a dogma and declared it to be the eternal truth. Another man did the same thing; then the two began to hate each other with an unholy hatred, each trying to impose his private scheme of the universe upon the other, and that is an epitome of some of the blackest pages of history. Against those old sectarians who substituted intolerance for charity, persecution for friendship, and did not love God because they hated their neighbors, Masonry made perpetual protest in a voice which is now becoming the eloquence of the world. A vast change of heart is now taking place in the religious world, by reason of an exchange of thought and courtesy and a closer personal touch, and the various sects, so long estranged, are learning to unite upon the things most worth while and the least open to debate. That is to say, they are moving toward the Masonic position, and when they arrive Masonry will preside over a scene which she prophesied from the beginning.

At last, in the not distant future, the old and bitter feuds of the sects will come to an end. Our little systems will have their day and cease to be, lost in the vision of a truth so great that all men are one in their littleness; one in their victorious assurance of "the ultimate decency of things, and the kindness of the veiled Father of men." Then men of every creed will ask, when they meet:

> "Not what is your creed?
> But what is your need?"

What is your vision of the meaning of this infinite universe, luminous and dark, glorious and terrible, in which we live? Then Masonry, having fulfilled a part of its sublime and prophetic mission upon earth, will rejoice. High above all dogmas that bind, all bigotries that blind, all bitterness that divides, it will write the eternal verities of the Fatherhood of God, the brotherhood of man, the moral law, the Golden Rule, and the hope of a life everlasting!

II

Out of this simple faith grows the philosophy which Masonry teaches in signs and symbols, in pictures and parables. Stated freely, stated sympathetically, it is that behind the pageant of nature, in it and over it, there is a Supreme Mind which initiates, impels, and controls all. That behind the life of man and its pathetic story in history, in it and over it, there is a righteous will, the intelligent conscience of the Most High. In short, that the first and last thing in the universe is mind, that the highest and deepest thing is conscience, and that the final reality is the absoluteness of love. Higher than that faith cannot fly; deeper than that thought cannot go.

There is but one real alternative of this philosophy. It is not atheism, because the adherents of atheism are too few, and its intellectual position is too precarious ever to be a menace. An atheist is an orphan, a waif wandering the midnight streets of time, homeless and alone. Nor is the alternative agnosticism, which in the nature of things can be only a passing mood of thought, when, indeed, it is not a confession of intellectual bankruptcy or a labor-saving device to escape the toil and fatigue of high thinking. It trembles in perpetual hesitation, like the donkey equidistant between two bundles of hay, starving to death but unable to make a decision. No, the real alternative is materialism, which played so large a part in scholarly circles fifty years ago, and which, defeated there, has betaken itself to the field of opportunity and practical affairs. This is the dread alternative of a denial of faith, a blight which would apply a sponge to all the high aspirations and ideals of our race. According to this dogma, the last things in the universe are atoms, their number, dance, combination, and growth. All mind, all will, all emotion, all character, all love is incidental, transitory, vain. The sovereign fact is mud, the final reality is dirt!

Against this horror Masonry has in every age stood as a witness for the soul. In the war of the mind against dust, in the choice between dirt and Deity, it has allied itself on the side of the great idealisms and optimisms of humanity. It takes the spiritual view of life and the world as being most in accord with the facts of experience, the promptings of right reason, the voice of conscience, and the vision of the soul. It dares to read the meaning of the universe through what is highest in human nature, not through what is lower; to assert that the soul is akin to an eternal spirit, and therefore deathless as God its Father is deathless. Think of what it means to say that. It means that what a man thinks, the manner of his feeling, the character of his activity and career are of vital and ceaseless concern to the eternal God. It means that we are not shapes of mud placed here by chance, but sons of the Most High, citizens of eternity, and that there is laid upon us an abiding obligation to live in a manner befitting the dignity and worth of the soul.

Here is a philosophy which lights up the world like a sunrise, evolving meaning out of mystery, and hope out of what would else be despair. It brings out the colors of human life, investing our fleeting mortal years—brief at their longest, broken at their best—with enduring significance and beauty. It gives each of us, however humble and obscure, a place and a part in the stupendous historical enterprise; makes us fellow workers with the Eternal in His redemptive making of humanity, and binds us to do His will upon earth as it is done in heaven. It subdues the intellect; it touches the heart; it begets in the will that sense of self-respect without which high and heroic living cannot be. Such is the philosophy upon which Masonry rests; and from it flow those bright streams that wander through and water this human world of ours.

III

Because this is so; because the human soul is akin to God and is endowed with powers to which no one may set a limit, it is and of right ought to be free. Thus, by the logic of its philosophy, not less than by the inspiration of its faith, Masonry has been impelled to make its historic demand for liberty of conscience, for the freedom of the intellect, and for the right of all men to stand erect, unfettered, and unafraid, equal before God and the law, each respecting the rights of his fellows. What we have to remember is, that before this truth found embodiment in any political constitution it was embedded in the will of God and the constitution of the human soul. If the Magna Charta demanded rights which government can grant, Masonry from the first asserted those inalienable rights of man derived from God the Father of man. Nor will it ever swerve one jot or tittle from its ancient and eloquent demand till all men, everywhere, are free in body, mind, and soul.

Never did this truth find sweeter voice than in the tones of the old Scotch fiddle on which Robert Burns, a Master Mason, sang, in lyric glee, of the sacredness of humanity, and the native divinity of human nature as the only lawful basis of society and the state. That music, heard long before in every Masonic lodge, went marching on, striding over continents, and trampling kingdoms down until it took form in the Declaration of Independence and Constitution of this republic, over whose birth Masonry presided and with whose growth it has had so much to do. It was not an accident that the Boston Tea Party, with its protest against taxation without representation, was planned in a Masonic lodge and executed by its members. Nor should we forget that the convention which framed our Constitution, with four men absent, could have been opened in form as a Masonic lodge. The fathers of this nation, inspired by Masonry, dared to assert the divine right of man to "life, liberty, and the pursuit of happiness, to secure which governments are instituted among men, deriving their just powers from the consent of the governed."

So it has been all through our national history—of which, if you are not proud, you ought to have public prayers said for you next Sunday—and to-day this great order, with its plea for liberty, equality, and fraternity, is worth more for the safety and sanctity of this republic than both its army and its navy. At every turn of events, when the rights of man have been threatened by enemies open and obvious, or subtle and insidious, Masonry has stood guard. In time of conflict she has softened the horrors of war, and in time of peace her altar light has shone as a signal fire along the heights of liberty, keeping watch over the principles wrought out by the blood and prayers and tears of our fathers. Not only in our own land, but everywhere over the broad earth, when men have thrown off the yoke of tyranny and demanded the rights that belong to manhood, they have found a friend in the Masonic order. Nor must we be less alert and vigilant to-day when, free of the danger of foes from without, our republic is imperiled by the negligence of indifference, the seduction of luxury, and the shadow of a passion-clouded, impatient discontent, whose end is madness and folly.

> "Love thou thy land, with love far-brought
> From out the storied past, and used
> Within the present, but transfused
> Through future time by power of thought."

Some day, when the cloud of prejudice has been dispelled by the searchlight of truth, the world will honor Masonry for its heroic service to freedom of thought and the liberty of faith. No part of its ministry has been more noble, no principle of its teaching has been more precious than its age-long and unwavering demand for the right and duty of every soul to seek that light by which no man was ever injured and that truth which makes man free. Down through the ages —often when the highest crime was not murder, but thinking, and when the human conscience was dragged as a slave at the wheel of the ecclesiastical chariot—always and everywhere Masonry has stood for the right of the soul to know the truth and to look up unhindered from the lap of earth into the face of Him in whose great hand it stands. Not freedom from faith, but freedom of faith, has been its watchword, on the ground that as despotism is the mother of anarchy, so bigoted dogmatism is the prolific source of skepticism.

Against those who would fetter thought in order to perpetuate an effete authority, who would give the skinny hand of the past a scepter to rule the aspiring and prophetic present, and seal the lips of living thinkers with the dicta of dead scholastics, Masonry will never ground arms. Her plea is for government without tyranny and religion without superstition, and as surely as the suns rise and set her fight will be crowned with victory. She fights not with force, still less with intrigue, but with the power of truth, the persuasions of reason, and the might of gentleness, seeking not to destroy her enemies but to win them to the liberty of the truth and the fellowship of love.

IV

For, if there be a God at all, who is the life of all that was, is, and is to be, that God must be the Father of all mankind; and if we are all born into this world by one high wisdom and one vast love, then we are brothers to the last man of us, forever. For better for worse, for richer for poorer, in sickness and in health, till death do us part, men are held together by ties of spiritual kinship, sons of one eternal Father. Upon this spiritual fact must rest every real human fraternity, and it is the basis of the age-old plea of Masonry not only for freedom, but for friendship among men. And, though long delayed—

> "It's comin' yet for a' that,
>   And man to man, the world o'er,
> Shall brothers be for a' that."

Our human history, saturated with blood and blistered with tears, is the story of man making friends with man. Society has evolved from a feud into a friendship by the slow growth of love and the welding of man first to his kin, and then to his kind. The first men who lived in the red dawn of time lived every man for himself, his heart a sanctuary of suspicions, every man feeling that every other man was his foe, and therefore his prey. So there was war, strife, and bloodshed. Slowly there came to the savage a gleam of the truth that it is better to help than to hurt, and he organized clans and tribes. But tribes were divided by rivers and mountains, and the men on one side of the river felt that the men on the other side were their enemies. Again there was war, pillage, and sorrow. Great empires arose and met in the shock of conflict, leaving a trail of skeletons across the earth. Then came the great roads, reaching out with their stony clutch and bringing the ends of the earth together. Men met, mingled, passed, and repassed, and learned that human nature is much the same everywhere, with hopes and fears in common. Still there were many things to divide and estrange men from each other, and the earth was full of bitterness.

Not satisfied with natural barriers, men erected high walls of sect and caste to exclude their fellows, and the men of one sect were sure that the men of all other sects were wrong—and would be lost. Thus, when real mountains no longer estranged man from man, mountains were made out of molehills—mountains of immemorial misunderstanding not yet moved into the sea. Barriers of race, of creed, of caste, of habit, of training, and interest separate men to-day, as if some malign genius were bent on keeping man from his fellows, begetting suspicion, uncharitableness, and hate. All through the ages men were unfriendly, and, therefore, unjust and cruel, largely because they were unacquainted.

> "Here lies the tragedy of our race;
> Not that men are poor;
> All men know something of poverty;
> Not that men are wicked;
> Who can claim to be good?
> Not that men are ignorant;
> Who can boast that he is wise?
> But that men are strangers."

In the meantime—and, verily, it was a mean time—Masonry, the oldest and most widely spread order, was toiling in behalf of friendship, uniting men upon the only basis upon which they can ever meet with dignity, each lodge an oasis of equality and good-will in a desert of feud and strife. At its altar men met as man to man, without vanity and without pretense, without fear and without reproach, held together by common vows to the right, as tourists crossing the Alps tie themselves together, so that if one slip and fall all may hold him up. Its tie of friendship—peculiar, particular, and unique—was like those tiny fibers running through the glaciers, along which sunbeams journey, melting the frozen mass and sending it to the valleys below in rivulets of blessing. Other fibers were there, but none more far-ramifying, none more tender, none more responsive to the light than the mystical tie of Masonic love. No tongue can tell the meaning of that gentle tie binding men together, no pen can trace the influences that traveled along it, melting the hardness of the world into pity.

Toward a great friendship, long foreseen by Masonic faith, the world is slowly moving, amid difficulties and delays; and to-day the sun looks down and sees men everywhere getting together, as though the race were fast becoming a vast league of sympathy and service. Of that day, which will surely come, when nations will be reverent in the use of freedom, just in the exercise of power, humane in the practice of wisdom; when no man will ride over the rights of his fellows; when no woman will be made forlorn, no little child wretched, by bigotry or greed, Masonry has ever been a prophet. Nor will she be content until the various threads of human fellowship are woven into one mystic cord of friendship, encircling the earth and holding the race in unity of spirit and the bonds of peace, as in the will of God it is one in origin, history, and end. Having outlived empires and philosophies, having seen generations appear and vanish, she will yet live to see the travail of her soul, and be satisfied—

> "When the war-drum throbs no longer,
>   And the battle flags are furled;
> In the parliament of man,
>   The federation of the world."

V

The Mission of Masonry! Years have fled, like hooded figures in hurried march, since our fathers set up their altar on the frontier, kindled its light and fell asleep, but the spirit and purpose of this ancient order remained. The forms of beauty into which the earth is rushing to-day are not the forms that greeted their eyes in 1840; the aspect of the sky has changed a thousand times since their eager and faithful vision looked up into it. Time has swept us on the wave of advance into a new world with wider horizons, mightier aspirations, and vaster obligations. But life is the same, unchangeable save for its onward march, the earth abideth, and the sky, though like a fleeting tent, is built anew after the same eternal model. Just so, though the forms of life alter, and new times demand new methods, the truths of faith and immutable duty of doing good abide.

The Mission of Masonry! He who would describe that must be a poet, a musician, and a seer—a master of melodies, echoes, and long, far-sounding cadences. Now, as always, it toils to make man better, to refine his thought and purify his dream, to broaden his outlook, to lift his altitude, to establish in amplitude and resoluteness his life in all its relations. All its great history, its vast accumulations of tradition, its simple faith and its solemn rites, its freedom and its friendship, are dedicated to a high moral ideal, seeking to tame the tiger in man and bring all his wild passions into obedience to the will of God. Unwearyingly it holds aloft, in picture and in dream, that temple of character which it is the noblest labor of life to build in the midst of the years, and which will outlast time and death. It has no other mission than to exalt and ennoble humanity, to bring light out of darkness, beauty out of angularity; to make every hard-won inheritance more secure, every sanctity more sacred, every hope more radiant.

The Mission of Masonry! When the spirit of this order has its way upon earth, as at last it certainly will, society will be a vast league of sympathy and justice, business a system of human service, law a rule of beneficence; the home will be more holy, the laughter of childhood more joyous, and the temple of prayer mortised and tenoned in simple faith. Evil, injustice, bigotry, and greed, and every vile and slimy thing that defiles humanity will skulk into the dark, unable to endure the light of a juster, wiser, more merciful order. Industry will be upright, education prophetic, and religion not a shadow, but a real presence, when man has become acquainted with man and has learned to worship God by serving his fellows. When Masonry is victorious every tyranny will fall, every bastile crumble, and man will be not only unfettered in mind and hand, but free of heart to walk erect in the light and dignity of the truth.

Such is the ideal, and by as much as are true to it, by so much are we loyal to the benign Mission of Masonry upon the earth. Fidelity to all that is holy demands that we give ourselves to it, trusting the power of truth, the reality of love, and the sovereign worth of character. For only as we incarnate this vision in actual life and activity does it become real, tangible, and effective. God works for man through man and seldom, if at all, in any other way. He asks for your voice and mine to speak His truth to man, for your hand and mind to do His work here below—sweet voices and clean hands to work His will and make liberty and love prevail over injustice and hate. The most precious wealth in the world is the wealth of established character; it makes all our moral currency valid. Not all of us can be learned or famous, but each of us can be pure of heart, undefiled by evil, undaunted by error, noble and true, faithful and useful to our fellow souls. Life is a capacity for the highest things. Let us make it a pursuit of the highest—an eager, incessant quest of truth, a noble utility, a genuine worth, a lofty honor, a wise freedom—that through us the Mission of Masonry may be yet further advanced.

> "I go mine, thou goest thine;
>   Many ways we wend,
> Many ways and many days,
>   Ending in one end.
> Many a wrong and its crowning song,
>   Many a road and many an inn,
> Far to roam, but only one home,
>   For all the world to win."

Chapter III

THE MINISTRY OF MASONRY[1]

Something in this scene, something in the words of my dear friend, appeals to me very deeply. So gracious a greeting evokes feelings beyond my words, and I understand what Lord Tennyson must have felt when, looking out upon the sea and listening to its voices, he cried:

> "I would that some tongue could utter
> The thoughts that arise in me."

Once upon a time, as my friend has said, I tried to talk to you as best I could on the Mission of Masonry, its faith, its philosophy, its demand for freedom, and its plea for universal friendship.

But the more I brood over the mystery of this order, its history, its genius, its possibilities of ministry to the higher human life, the more the wonder grows, the higher the horizon, and the longer the vistas that unfold. Let me beseech you, then, to lend me your hearts while I tell

[1] Address delivered before the Grand Lodge of Iowa at its 70th Annual Communication at Council Bluffs, June 10. 1913.

you a little more of the meaning of Masonry as it has grown up in my heart. Studying Masonry is like looking at a sunrise; each man who looks is filled with the beauty and glory of it, but the splendor is not diminished. Over all alike its ineffable wonder falls, subduing the mind, softening the heart, and exalting the life.

I

The better to make vivid what lies in my heart, let me recall a scene from one of the great books of the world, *War and Peace,* by Count Tolstoi —a name that should be spoken with reverence wherever men assemble in the name of good-will. He was, if we except Lincoln, the tallest soul, the most picturesque and appealing figure who walked under our human sky in the last century. This book, the greatest of its kind known to literature, makes one think of a giant playing with mountains, tossing them to and fro as though they were toys—so powerful is it, so vast in its sweep, so vivid in its panorama. Its heroine is a whole nation—the beautiful, strange, tormented land of Russia. We see its lights and shadows, its wide expanse, and its quiet hamlets; its people at work and play, in peace and war—now hovering like a shadow on the heels of their enemies, now fleeing in terror in the glare of their burning cities. What a picture of the tumult of a nation, and the vicissitudes of life, in the light of the Napoleonic invasion!

One of the arresting figures of the story is Count Pierre Bezuhov—in whom Tolstoi has shown us one side of his own soul, as in Prince Andre he has unveiled the other. Pierre is the richest man in Russia, owning vast estates, including both the land and the serfs on the land. Like so many young noblemen of his day, he has lived a wild, sensual, dissolute life, careless alike of the rights and wrongs of his fellows. He was married to a beautiful, bewitching, sensual woman, whose paramour he has just killed in a duel. On his way to St. Petersburg he falls in with an old man, simply dressed, but with the light of a great peace in his face. The stranger addresses the Count and tells him that he has heard of his misfortune, referring to the duel resulting in the death at his hands of the lover of his wife. He is aware, too, as he goes on to say, of the wild, sin-bespattered life the Count has lived, of his way of thinking, of his pride, indolence, and ignorance. The Count listened to these severe words, he hardly knew why—perhaps because he heard in them an undertone of sympathy. the accent of a great pity, and what he heard in the voice he saw in the kindly face.

On the hand of the old man the Count noticed

a ring, and in it the emblem of the order here assembled. He asked the stranger if he was not a Mason. Whereupon the old man, looking searchingly into the eyes of the Count, said that he belonged to that order, in whose name he extended to him the hand of a brother man, in the name of God the Father. At the mention of the name of God a smile curled on the lips of the Count, who said:

"I ought to tell you that I don't believe in God." The old Freemason smiled as a rich man, holding millions in his hand, might smile at a poor wretch.

"Yes, you do not know Him, sir," said the stranger. "You do not know Him, that is why you are unhappy. But He is here, He is within me, He is in thee, and even in these scoffing words you have just uttered. If He is not, we should not be speaking of Him, sir. Whom dost thou deny? How came there within thee the conception that there is such an incomprehensible Being?"

Something in the venerable stranger, who spoke earnestly, as one who stood in the light of a vision, touched the Count deeply, and stirred in him a longing to see what the old man saw and to know what he knew. Abject, hopeless, haunted by an ill-spent life, with the blood of a fellow man on his hands—his eyes betrayed his longing to know God. Though he did not speak, the kindly eyes of the stranger read his face and answered his unasked question:

"He exists, but to know Him is hard. It is not attained by reason, but by life. The highest truth is like the purest dew. Can I hold in an impure vessel that pure dew and judge of its purity? Only by inner purification can we know Him."

Finally, the old man asked the young nobleman if he would not like to look into the mysteries of Masonry. Not so much what the stranger had said as what he was—his gentle, austere, benign spirit, that had in it something of the Fatherhood of God—made the Count say, "Yes." The stranger asked him to report at a certain room in St. Petersburg, where he would be introduced to those high in authority among Freemasons. Meanwhile, what the gently stern old man had said sank into the soul of the hitherto heedless young nobleman; and when he reported at the lodge room and was asked, as every man is asked, the one indispensable question: "Do you believe in God?"—something deeper than his doubts, something higher than his skepticism spoke within him, and he answered, *"Yes."*

There follows a detailed description of his initiation, which those who are not Masons may be curious to read. Unfortunately, it tells them nothing of what takes place in a lodge room on such occasions; but it will show them the spirit that lives and glows on the altar of Masonry. No one but a Mason could have written it; and while the chain of evidence is not quite complete, I am safe in saying that, as with Count Pierre in the story, so with Count Tolstoi himself, it was Masonry which first lifted him out of the pit of atheism and sensualism, set his feet upon the Rock of Ages, and started him toward the city of God. Does this not suggest to us the deeper meaning of Masonry, its higher ministry, and the service it may render to the inner life of man?

II

What is Masonry? What is it trying to teach? What does it seek to do? Above all, what can it do for the man who receives it into his heart, loves it, and lives in the light of it? What profound ministry may it render to the young man who enters its temple in the morning of life, when the dew is on his days and the birds are singing in his heart? Let me try to answer these questions this summer afternoon in the spirit of Count Tolstoi, who must hereafter be numbered with those prophets and bards—with poets like Goethe and Burns, musicians like Mozart, patriots like Mazzini and Washington—who loved this historic order. Such names shine like stars in the crown of humanity, and none with truer luster than that of Tolstoi, who was a teacher of purity, pity, and peace among men.

Time out of mind Masonry has been defined as a system of morality, veiled in allegory, and illustrated by symbols. That is so far true—far enough, indeed, to describe a world-encircling fellowship and its far-ramifying influence. But it is not of the extent of Masonry that I wish to speak this afternoon, but, rather, of its depth —its service to the lonely inner life of man where the issues of character and destiny are determined for good or ill. No more worthy purpose can inspire any order than the earnest, active endeavor to bring men—first the individual man, and then, so far as possible, those united with him—to a deeper, richer fellowship with spiritual reality. Since this is the purpose of Masonry, let us inquire as to what it is, whence it came, and how it seeks to reach the souls of men where the real battles of life are fought, now with shouts of victory, now with sobs of defeat.

It is true that Masonry is not a religion, still less a cult, but it has religiously preserved some things of highest importance to religion—among them the right of each individual soul to its own religious faith. Holding aloof from separate sects and creeds, it has taught all of them to respect and tolerate each other; asserting a principle broader than any of them—the sanctity of the soul and the duty of every man to revere, or at least to regard with charity, what is sacred to his fellows. Our order is like the crypts underneath the old cathedrals—a place where men of every creed, who long for something deeper and truer, older and newer than they have hitherto known, meet and unite. Having put away childish things, they find themselves made one by a profound and child-like faith, each bringing down into that quiet crypt his own pearl of great price—

"The Hindu his innate disbelief in this world, and his unhesitating belief in another world; the Buddhist his perception of an eternal law, his submission to it, his gentleness, his pity; the Mohammedan, if nothing else, his sobriety; the Jew his clinging, through good and evil days, to the one God, who loveth righteousness and whose name is 'I AM'; the Christian, that which is better than all, if those who doubt it would only try it—our love of God, call Him what you will, manifested in our love of man, our love of the living, our love of the dead, our living and undying love. Who knows but that the crypt of the past may yet become the church of the future?"

There have been great secret orders, like that represented here to-day, since recorded history began; and no man may ever hope to estimate their service to our race. In every age, in every civilized land—from the priests of Isis on yonder side of the Pyramids, to the orders of Eleusis and Mithras in Greece and Rome—we trace their silent, far-reaching influence and power. The *Mysteries,* said Plato, were established by men of great genius who, in the early ages, strove to teach purity, to ameliorate the cruelty of the race, to refine its manners and morals, and to restrain society by stronger bonds than those which human laws impose. Cicero bears a like witness to the high aim of the same mystic orders in his day. Thus in ages of darkness, of complexity, of conflicting peoples, tongues, and faiths, these great orders toiled in behalf of friendship, bringing men together under the banner of faith, and training them for a nobler moral life.

No mystery any longer attaches to what those orders taught, but only as to what particular rites, dramas, and symbols were used by them in their ceremonies. They taught faith in a God above, in the moral law within, heroic purity of soul, austere discipline of character, justice, piety, and the hope of a life beyond death. Tender and tolerant of all faiths, they formed an all-embracing moral and spiritual fellowship which rose above barriers of nation, race, and creed, satisfying the craving of men for unity, while evoking in them a sense of that eternal mysticism out of which all religions were born. Their ceremonies, so far as we know them, were stately and moving dramas of the moral life and the fate of the soul. Mystery and secrecy added impressiveness, and fable and enigma disguised in imposing spectacle the simple, familiar, everlasting laws of justice, piety, and a hope of immortality. As Cicero said, the initiates of the *Mysteries* not only received lessons which made life tolerable, but drew from their rites happy hopes for the hour of death.

Masonry stands in this tradition; and if we may not say that it is historically related to those great ancient orders, it is their spiritual descendant, and renders the same ministry to our age which the *Mysteries* rendered to the olden world. It is, indeed, no other than those same historic orders in disguise; the same stream of sweetness and light flowing in our day—like the fabled river Alpheus which, gathering the waters of a hundred rills along the hillsides of Arcadia, sank, lost to light, in a chasm in the earth, only to reappear in the fountain of Arethusa. Apart from its rites, there is no mystery in Masonry, save the mystery of all great and simple things. So far from being hidden and occult, its glory lies in its openness, its emphasis upon the realities which are to our human world what air and sunlight are to nature. Its secret is of so great and simple a kind that it is easily overlooked; its mystery too obvious to be found out.

Our age resembles in many ways the age which saw the introduction into the world of the teachings of Jesus. To one who regards mankind with tenderness, a time like this is full of hope, but full of many perils also. Men are confused, troubled, and strangely alone. Anything is possible. Forms of faith are changing, and many are bewildered—as witness the number of those running to and fro, following every wandering light, and falling, often, into the bogs of fanaticism. Oh, the pathos of it! A strange indifference has settled over the world, but underneath it there is a profound, unsatisfied hunger. There is a mood to-day which soon will utter a cry, and it will be a cry for a more vivid sense of God: that is our hope. Yet that cry may fling many a soul upon the bosom of doubt and despair: that is our fear. Amidst this peril, Masonry brings men together at the altar of prayer, keeps alive faith in the truths that make us men, seeking, by every resource of art, to make tangible the power of love, the worth of beauty, and the reality of the ideal. Who can measure such a ministry, who can describe it!

III

Let me strive to make it all more vivid by recalling a parable translated by Max Muller from the lore of the East. The gods, having stolen from man his divinity, met in council to discuss where they should hide it. One suggested that it be carried to the other side of the earth and buried; but it was pointed out that man is a great wanderer, and that he might find the lost treasure on the other side of the earth. Another proposed that it be dropped into the depths of the sea; but the same fear was expressed—that man, in his insatiable curiosity, might dive deep enough to find it even there. Finally, after a space of silence, the oldest and wisest of the gods said: "Hide it in man himself, as that is the last place he will ever think to look for it." And it was so agreed, all seeing at once its subtle and wise strategy.

Man wandered over the earth for ages, searching in all places, high and low, far and near, before he thought to look within himself for the divinity he sought. At last, slowly, dimly, he began to realize that what he thought was far off, hidden in "the pathos of distance," is nearer than the breath he breathes, even in his own heart. Here lies the deepest ministry of Masonry —that it makes a young man aware of the divinity that is within him, wherefrom his whole life takes beauty and meaning, and inspires him to follow and obey it. No hour in life is more solemn and revealing than that in which a man learns that what he seeks he has already found, else he would not be seeking it. Once a man learns that deep secret, life is new, and the old world is a valley all dewy to the dawn, aglow with beauty and athrill with melody.

There never was a truer saying than that of Thomas Carlyle when he said that the religion of a man is the chief fact concerning him. By religion he meant, as he went on to explain, not the creed to which a man will subscribe or otherwise give his assent; not that necessarily; often not that at all—since we see men of all degrees of worth and worthlessness signing all kinds of creeds. No, the religion of a man is that which he practically believes, lays to heart, acts upon, and knows concerning this mysterious universe and his duty and destiny in it. That is in all cases the primary thing in him, and creatively determines all the rest; that is his religion. It is, then, of vital importance what faith, what vision, what conception of life a man lays to heart and acts upon. It is as a man thinks in his heart whether life be worth while or not, and whether the world be luminous or dark.

Let me show you that this is so. Optimists

and pessimists live in the same world, walk under the same sky, and observe the same facts. Skeptics and believers look up at the same great stars —the stars that shone in Eden and will flash again in Paradise. Thomas Hardy and George Meredith were contemporaries and friends—one looking out over a dismal, shadow-haunted Egdon heath, under a sky as gray as a tired face; the other a citizen of a world all dipped in hues of sunrise and sunset, with a lark-song over it! Clearly, the difference in all these cases is a difference not of fact, but of faith; of insight, outlook, and point of view—a difference of inner attitude and habit of thought with regard to the worth of life and the meaning of the world. By the same token, any influence which reaches and alters that inner habit and bias of mind, and changes it from doubt to faith, from fear to courage, from despair to sunburst hope, has wrought the most vital and benign ministry which a mortal may enjoy in the midst of the years.

Every man, as each of you can testify, has a train of thought on which he rides when he is alone. The dignity and nobility of his life, as well as its happiness, depend upon the direction in which that train is going, the baggage it carries, and the scenery through which it travels. If, then, Masonry can put that inner train of thought on the right track, freight it with precious baggage, and start it on the way to the city of God, what other or higher service can it render to a man? That is just what it does for any man who will give himself to it, bringing to him from afar the old wisdom-religion—that simple, pure, and lofty truth wrought out through ages of experience, tested by time, and found to be valid for the life of man. Whoso lays that lucid and profound wisdom to heart, and acts upon it, will have little to regret, and nothing to fear, when the evening shadows fall.

High, fine, ineffably rich, and beautiful is the faith and vision which Masonry gives to those who foregather at its altar. By such teaching, if they have the heart to heed it, men become wise, knowing that all evil ways have been often tried and found wanting. By it they learn how to be both brave and gentle, faithful and firm; how to renounce superstition and yet retain faith; how to keep a fine poise of reason between the falsehood of extremes; how to accept the joys of life with glee, and endure its ills with patient valor; how to look upon the folly of man and not forget his nobility—in short, how to live cleanly, kindly, calmly, opened-eyed, and unafraid in a sane world, sweet of heart and full of hope. It may not be a substitute for religion, but he who makes it a law of his life, loves it, and obeys it, will be most ready to receive the great passwords of religious faith. Happy the young man who in the morning of his years takes this simple and high wisdom as his guide, philosopher, and friend!

IV

Such is the ministry of Masonry to the individual—lifting him out of the mire and setting his feet in the long, white path marked out by the footsteps of ages; and through the individual it serves society and the state. If by some art one could trace those sweet, invisible influences which move to and fro like shuttles in a loom, weaving the net-work of laws, reverences, sanctities, which make the warp and woof of society —giving to statutes their dignity and power, to the gospel its opportunity, to the home its canopy of peace and beauty, to the young an enshrinement of inspiration, and the old a mantle of protection; if one had the pen of an angel then might one tell the story of what Masonry has done for Iowa. No wonder George Eliot said that eloquence is but a ripple on the bosom of the unspoken and the unspeakable!

What is it that so tragically delays the march of man toward that better social order whereof our prophets dream? Our age and land are full of schemes of every kind for the reform and betterment of mankind. Why do they not succeed? Some fail, perhaps, because they are imprudent and ill-considered, in that they expect too much of human nature and do not take into account the stubborn facts of life. But why does not the wisest and noblest plan do half what its devisers hope and pray and labor to bring about? Because there are not enough men fine enough of soul, large enough of sympathy, noble enough of nature to make the dream come true. So that when Masonry, instead of identifying itself with particular schemes of reform, devotes all its benign energy to refining and ennobling the souls of men, she is doing fundamental work in behalf of all high enterprises. By as much as she succeeds, every noble cause succeeds; if she fails, everything fails!

Recall what was passing before the eyes of men in this land fifty years ago to-day. What gloom, what uncertainty, what anxiety—Gettysburg less than a month away! The very life of the republic hung in the balance! Think of those first three days of July, 1863, when fifty-four thousand young men, the flower of our future, lay dead and wounded—piled in heaps of blue and gray, quivering with pain, their white faces turned to the sky! Nor was that all. Far away in northern towns and southern hamlets, sad-faced women heard, now with shrieks, now with dumb, unutterable woe, the long roll-call of the dead! What man who has a heart, or who cares for the future of his race, does not pray that such scenes may never again be witnessed on this earth! What can prevent a repetition of the horrors of war? Nothing but the growth in the hearts of men of the spirit of justice, freedom, and friendship which Masonry seeks, quietly, to evoke and inspire! If our fathers had known each other in the sixties as we know each other to-day, there would have been no Civil War! So it will be the world over, when man comes to know his fellow men as he learns to know them and love them at the altar of this order. Then shall be fulfilled the song of those who sang of "peace on earth *among men of good-will!*"

Again, no one need be told that we are on the eve, if not in the midst, of a stupendous and bewildering revolution of social and industrial life. It shakes England to-day. It makes France tremble to-morrow. It will alarm Germany next week. The questions in dispute can never be settled in an air of hostility. If they are settled at all, and settled right, it must be in an atmosphere of mutual recognition and respect such as that which Masonry strives to create and make prevail. Whether it be a conflict of nations, or a clash of class with class, appeal must be made to intelligence and the moral sense, as befits the dignity of man. Amidst bitterness and strife Masonry brings men of capital and labor, men of every rank and walk of life together as men, and nothing else, at an altar where they can talk and not fight, discuss and not dispute, and each may learn the point of view of his fellows. Other hope there is none save in this spirit of friendship and fairness, of democracy and the fellowship of man with man.

Even so it is in religion—that kingdom of faith and hope and prayer so long defamed by bigotry and distracted by sectarian feud. How many fine minds have been estranged from the altar of faith because they were required to believe what it was impossible for them to believe—and, rather than sacrifice their integrity, they turned away from the last place from which a man should ever turn away. No part of the ministry of Masonry is more beautiful and wise than its appeal, not for tolerance, but for fraternity; not for uniformity, but for unity of spirit amidst varieties of outlook and opinion. God be thanked for one altar where no one is asked to surrender his liberty of thought and become an indistinguishable atom in a mass of sectarian agglomeration. What a witness to the worth of an order that it brings together men of all faiths in behalf of those truths which are greater than all sects, deeper than all dogmas—the glory and the hope of man!

When is a man a Mason? When he can look out over the rivers, the hills, and the far horizon with a profound sense of his own littleness in the vast scheme of things, and yet have faith, hope, and courage. When he knows that down in his heart every man is as noble, as vile, as divine, as diabolic, and as lonely as himself, and seeks to know, to forgive, and to love his fellow man. When he knows how to sympathize with men in their sorrows, yea, even in their sins— knowing that each man fights a hard fight against many odds. When he has learned how to make friends and to keep them, and above all how to keep friends with himself. When he loves flowers, can hunt the birds without a gun, and feels the thrill of an old forgotten joy when he hears the laugh of a little child. When he can be happy and high-minded amid the meaner drudgeries of life. When star-crowned trees and the glint of sunlight on flowing waters subdue him like the thought of one much loved and long dead. When no voice of distress reaches his ears in vain, and no hand seeks his aid without response. When he finds good in every faith that helps any man to lay hold of higher things, and to see majestic meanings in life, whatever the name of that faith may be. When he can look into a wayside puddle and see something besides mud, and into the face of the most forlorn mortal and see something beyond sin. When he knows how to pray, how to love, how to hope. When he has kept faith with himself, with his fellow man, with his God; in his hand a sword for evil, in his heart a bit of a song—glad to live, but not afraid to die! In such a man, whether he be rich or poor, scholarly or unlearned, famous or obscure, Masonry has wrought her sweet ministry!

Chapter IV

THE GEOMETRY OF GOD: A MASONIC SERMON

"According to the measure of a man, that is, of the angel."—Rev. 21:17.

Few realize the service of the science of numbers to the faith of man in the morning of the world. It was almost his first hint of law and order in life when he sought to find some kind of key to the mighty maze of things. Living in the midst of change and seeming chance, he found in the laws of numbers a path by which to escape the awful sense of life as a series of accidents in the hands of a capricious Power. Surely it was not unnatural that a science whereby men obtained such glimpses of unity and order in the world should be sacred among them, imparting its form to their faith. Having revealed so much, numbers came to wear mystical meanings in a way quite alien to our prosaic habit of thinking—faith in our day having betaken itself to other symbols.

One of the first men to follow this hint was Pythagoras, of whom we know so little and would like to know so much. He was a lofty and noble figure, albeit half-hidden in myth, and only a few of his words have floated down to us. He saw in all the multiplicity of experience, to which Heraclitus had borne witness, a rhythmic march —a movement, but with disciplined step and the reasonable soul of music in it. One of his few sayings that remain sums up his vision: "All things are in numbers, the world is a living arithmetic in its development—a realized geometry in its repose." Take a snowflake and look at it under a glass, and you will see what filled that ancient thinker with wonder. It is an exquisite example of the geometry of God—squares, circles, triangles, pentagons, hexagons, parallelograms, more exact and delicate than the deftest hand could trace. Throw a stone into a still sheet of water, and immediately there arises an ever-widening series of concentric circles. The mountains in their strength stand fast forever, held in their places by a parallelogram of forces, and the stars swing round their vast orbits as noiselessly as a dewdrop is poised on a flower.

Such is the structure of the universe, and it is no wonder that Pythagoras saw in these signs and designs, everywhere present, the thought-forms of the Eternal Mind; else they would not be the natural, self-sought forms of matter.

Nature is a realm of numbers, and the frolic architecture of a snowflake is a lesson in geometry. Music moves with measured step, using geometrical figures, and cannot free itself from numbers without dying away into discord. From Pythagoras this insight passed to Plato, whose opulent genius gave eloquent exposition to the Doctrine of Numbers. When asked by a pupil what God does, he replied, "God geometrizes continually," and he was often wont to say that Geometry, rightfully understood, is the knowledge of the Eternal. Over the porch of his Academy at Athens he inscribed the words, "Let no one who is ignorant of Geometry enter my doors," meaning that his teaching rested upon the science of numbers. What Plato and Pythagoras saw modern science confirms in myriad ways, as we may read, for example, in the researches of Henri Fabre. In the last chapter of his book on *The Cufic of the Spider,* he wrote:

"Geometry, that is to say, the science of harmony in space, presides over everything. We find it in the arrangement of a fir-cone, as in the arrangement of an Epeira's living web; we find it in the spiral of a snail shell, in the chaplet of a spider's thread, and in the orbit of a planet; it is everywhere, as perfect in the world of atoms as in the world of immensities. And this universal geometry tells us of a Universal Geometrician, whose divine compass has measured all things."

How interesting it is, revealing the infinite ingenuity of the Divine imagination and the measured movements of its labors. Naturally we find hints of this science in the Bible, in which certain sacred numbers recur, indicating words, suggesting thoughts, and revealing truths. Nowhere is this more manifest than in the book of the Apocalypse, which, instead of being a series of clouded and confused visions, is a work of spiritual mathematics. In that book Three is the signature of Deity. Four indicates the world of created things. Seven denotes peace and covenant, while Ten is the symbol of completeness. Even numbers symbolize earthly things, odd numbers heavenly things, and the odd and even added unite the two. With this ancient science in mind, the vision of the City of God, with its geometrical design, takes a new meaning, albeit we should add to it the vision in the prophecy of Zechariah in which the young man is told that the holy city is not to be measured in cubits of human reckoning. Some hint of the paradox of the measurable and the immeasurable must have been in the mind of the Seer of Patmos, as if some one had asked him how our earthly cubits can form a calculus for that which knows not the

THE GEOMETRY OF GOD

gauge of time or space. Hence his parenthesis, to resolve the doubt, "according to the measure of a man, that is, of the angel."

Man is a citizen of two worlds, but he has no skill to realize the world of spirit apart from the aid of the world of sense. If he asks, wistfully, about the life to come, the only answer is one expressed in the images and colors of the life that now is. As often as he tries to ponder, reverently, what is the essential nature of God, he finds himself thinking of the Eternal in terms of those moral qualities which he sees, dimly enough, in the noblest men. He cannot help himself; there is no other way for him to think. Truth, justice, mercy, goodness in man, must be of the same nature as truth, justice and goodness in God, however they may differ in degree, else they mean nothing to us. Long ago Ovid said that "our measure is in our immortal souls," and our faith not less than our philosophy rests upon the fact that there is an angel in man, something akin to the Eternal, making our highest thought and vision valid. No doubt that was what Plato meant when he said that by the art of measurement the soul is saved—that is, by measuring up to the Angel within us we attain to the truth; by reading the reality of life through the highest, we learn its meaning and value. If so, we have our marching orders and the path of attainment is made plain even to the humblest, and no one need err therein or lose his way.

Just as in nature, from snowflake to star certain designs are found everywhere—circles, cubes, triangles—so, among all races and in all ages, certain ideas, ideals, faiths and hopes are held and trusted. Socrates made the discovery —one of the greatest ever made—that humanity is universal. By asking questions, which was the business of his life, he found that when men, whether they be artists or artisans, think round a problem and go to the bottom of it, they disclose a common nature and a common system of truth. After this manner the consensus of human insight, thought and experience confirms the fundamental truths of faith, like a problem of geometry, and we are justified in taking these basic ideas as the thought-forms of the Eternal Mind reflected in the mind of man. There is also a moral geometry which works itself out in the same way, tested by age-long and sorrowful human experience. Every evil way has been so often tried, that when we see a lad start along a dark path of evildoing we know what the result will be. No prophet is needed to predict the final issue; it is a problem in geometry. As David Swing said, in his noble sermon on "The Idealist," writing in his calm and simple manner:

"Some speak of ideals as if they were mere

dreams. On the opposite all high ideals are only life-like portraits seen in advance. It would be much more true to affirm that ideals are the most accurate results reached by the most painstaking calculations. It stands much in their favor that they have come not from the brains of the wicked, but from the intellects that were the greatest. The greatest men of each age have pleaded for Liberty, because only the greatest minds can paint in advance the picture of a free people. Many nations are in the dust and mire to-day, because they have no minds great enough to grasp a divine ideal. Instead of being a romance, a noble ideal is often the long mathematical calculation of a mind as logical as Euclid. Idealism is not the musings of a visionary; it is the calm geometry of life."

For the rest, let us consider in a practical way the geometry of manhood, its proportions and dimensions. Like the Holy City, which the Seer saw descending from heaven, its length and breadth and height must be equal, as Phillips Brooks taught in his great sermon on "The Symmetry of Life,"—which his church asked him to repeat ever so often. The basis of the triangle of character—that is to say, the length of a man, the extent of his influence and power, is a matter of morality. Purity is the first measure of a man. Lacking a certain simple, sturdy, homely, moral quality, he is a man only by the accident of his shape, though he have the learning of Bacon, the grace of Chesterfield, and the eloquence of Webster. Morals are ever the boundaries of liberty and the primary dimensions of manhood. Honesty, purity, truthfulness—nothing can take their place, and without them religion is either a superstition or a sham. A pure heart may sanctify a creed, but a creed, however true it may be, must bear moral fruit before it can sanctify a life. To give morality any other than the first place is to invert the order of life and upset all its values. It is the foundation of character and of society.

But a man may be moral, and yet mean. He may be clean, but cruel; righteous, but uncharitable; truthful, and yet narrow, bigoted and hard. He may throw a poor family out of his house for lack of rent, and in so doing be honest—and inhuman! If there is anything worse than the wrongs wrought by wicked men, it is the evil done by good men. That which gives beauty, breadth and mellowness to life, melting our morality into goodness, is sympathy. And so to purity we must add pity. Justice runs lengthwise of life, but mercy is width, and is an evidence of nobility, of refinement, of graciousness of spirit. Lacking it, we have a Calvin in the church consenting to the death of Servetus because of

THE GEOMETRY OF GOD

a difference of dogma, and a Jaubert in fiction pursuing like a sleuth hound the weary, tangled and sorrowful steps of Jean Valjean. Man is akin to the animal, but God put into his heart an alabaster box of pity out of which, when once it is opened, come the amenities of life, its courtesies, its graces, and those extensions of sympathy which it is the mission of culture, not less than of religion, to promote. And toleration, too, since heaven is only a village if it is made of only those thinkers who come always to the truth. Blessed be this broad and sunny sympathy in which bigotry and cynicism melt away and reveal to us the measure of man, that is, of the angel that is in him.

There is yet another measure of manhood, what William James called "that altogether other dimension of existence," so often forgotten in our day. Some, to be sure, regard it as a kind of fourth dimension, a thing which you may argue exists, but which we can never realize. Not so. No Mason, at least, can think so. It is a natural, normal development of man, without which his life lacks symmetry and is a thing unfinished and imperfect. Call it a mystical faith, if you will; from it we derive most of our ideal impulses, our aspirations that transcend the merely sensible and understandable world. From beyond ourselves comes that ray of white light which can brighten the pale moonlight into a glowing sunlight, give to the light of the sun a seven-fold brightness, and glorify all common things—as De Hooge lets the sunlight fall on the rubbish of a back yard and wakens in us a thrill of joy and wonder.

Men must seek the heights of being, must be tall of soul as well as broad, if they are to see life in the large. Altitude of mind gives new proportions and perspectives, and shows that many things of which men are wont to make much are insignificant, and that other things, like a cup of cool water offered a Brother, are of eternal moment. It is when we add this third dimension that we see that man, when measured by the Angel in him, is immeasurable. Man is the measure of all things, said an ancient sage; but man himself, in the higher reaches of his being, cannot be measured. He is like an inlet of the sea. Looking landward, it is limited; looking seaward, it is linked with the infinite. "I think God's thoughts after Him," said Kepler, as he looked through his glass into the sky, which is true of all high human thinking, all noble living, all upward-leaping aspiration. Truly, He that made us hath set eternity in our hearts, and restless we are until we find our rest in reunion with His will in which is our peace.

Let us strive, then, to unite purity, pity and

prayer in our lives, revealing the length and breadth and height of life. Also, let us judge life and our fellows by the Ideal of the Angel, that so, at last, when we are tested by the measure of the Angel—that is, by the Angel of Death—we may be found to have attained, in some degree, to the measure of the stature of true manhood. And by as much as we have failed, by so much let us trust the mercy of God which is without measure and knows no end—

> "For the love of God is broader
>   Than the measure of man's mind;
> And the heart of the Eternal
>   Is most wonderfully kind."

Chapter V

THE BIBLE IN MASONRY

Time is a river, and books are boats. Many volumes start down that stream, only to be wrecked and lost beyond recall in its sands. Only a few, a very few, endure the testings of time and live to bless the ages following. To-night we are met to pay homage to the greatest of all books—the one enduring Book which has traveled down to us from the far past, freighted with the richest treasure that ever any book has brought to humanity. What a sight it is to see five hundred men gathered about an open Bible—how typical of the spirit and genius of Masonry, its great and simple faith and its benign ministry to mankind.

No Mason needs to be told what a place of honor the Bible has in Masonry. One of the great Lights of the Order, it lies open upon the altar at the center of the lodge. Upon it every Mason takes solemn vows of love, of loyalty, of chastity, of charity, pledging himself to our tenets of Brotherly Love, Relief, and Truth. Think what it means for a young man to make such a covenant of consecration in the morning of life, taking that wise old Book as his guide, teacher and friend! Then as he moves forward from one degree to another, the imagery of the Bible becomes familiar and eloquent, and its mellow, haunting music sings its way into his heart.

And yet, like everything else in Masonry, the Bible, so rich in symbolism, is itself a symbol —that is, a part taken for the whole. It is a sovereign symbol of the Book of Faith, the Will of God as man has learned it in the midst of the years—that perpetual revelation of himself which God is making mankind in every land and every age. Thus, by the very honor which Masonry pays to the Bible, it teaches us to revere every book of faith in which men find help for to-day and hope for the morrow, joining hands with the man of Islam as he takes oath on the Koran, and with the Hindu as he makes covenant with God upon the book that he loves best.

For Masonry knows, what so many forget, that religions are many, but Religion is one— perhaps we may say one thing, but that one thing includes everything—the life of God in the soul of man, and the duty and hope of man which proceed from His essential character. Therefore it invites to its altar men of all faiths, knowing that, if they use different names for "the Nameless One of a hundred names," they are yet praying to the one God and Father of all; knowing, also, that while they read different volumes, they are in fact reading the same vast Book of the Faith of Man as revealed in the struggle and sorrow of the race in its quest of God. So that, great and noble as the Bible is, Masonry sees it as a symbol of that eternal Book of the Will of God which Lowell described when he wrote his memorable lines:

> "Slowly the Bible of the race is writ,
>   And not on paper leaves nor leaves of stone;
> Each age, each kindred, adds a verse to it,
>   Texts of despair or hope, of joy or moan.
> While swings the sea, while mists the mountain shroud,
> While thunder's surges burst on cliffs of cloud,
> Still at the prophets' feet the nations sit."

None the less, much as we honor every book of faith in which any man has found courage to lift his hand above the night that covers him and lay hold of the mighty Hand of God, with us the Bible is supreme. What Homer was to the Greeks, what the Koran is to the Arabs, that, and much more, the grand old Bible is to us. It is the mother in our literary family, and if some of its children have grown up and become wise in their own conceit, they yet rejoice to gather about its knee and pay tribute. Not only was the Bible the loom on which our language was woven, but it is a pervasive, refining, redeeming force bequeathed to us, with whatsoever else that is good and true, in the very fiber of our being. Not for a day do we regard the Bible simply as a literary classic, apart from what it means to the faiths and hopes and prayers of men, and its inweaving into the intellectual and spiritual life of our race.

There was a time when the Bible formed almost the only literature of England; and to-day, if it were taken away, that literature would be torn to tatters and shreds. Truly did Macaulay say that, if everything else in our language should perish, the Bible would alone suffice to show the whole range and power and beauty of our speech. From it Milton learned his majesty of song, and Ruskin his magic of prose. Carlyle had in his very blood, almost without knowing it, the rhapsody and passion of the prophets—their sense of the Infinite, of the littleness of man, of the sarcasm of Providence; as Burns, before him, had learned from the same fireside Book the indestructibleness of honor and the humane pity of God which throbbed in his lyrics of love and liberty. Thus, from Shakespeare to Tennyson, the Bible sings in our poetry, chants in our music, echoes in our eloquence, and in our tragedy flashes forever its truth of the terribleness of sin, the tenderness of God, and the inextinguishable hope of man.

My brethren, here is a Book whose scene is the sky and the dirt and all that lies between—a Book that has in it the arch of the heavens, the curve of the earth, the ebb and flow of the sea, sunrise and sunset, the peaks of mountains and the glint of sunlight on flowing waters, the shadow of forests on the hills, the song of birds and the color of flowers. But its two great characters are God and the Soul, and the story of their eternal life together is its one everlasting romance. It is the most human of books, telling the old forgotten secrets of the heart, its bitter pessimism and its death-defying hope, its pain, its passion, its sin, its sob of grief and its shout of joy—telling all, without malice, in its Grand Style which can do no wrong, while echoing the sweet-toned pathos of the pity and mercy of God. No other book is so honest with us, so mercilessly merciful, so austere yet so tender, piercing the heart, yet healing the deep wounds of sin and sorrow.

Take this great and simple Book, white with age yet new with the dew of each new morning, tested by the sorrowful and victorious experience of centuries, rich in memories and wet with the tears of multitudes who walked this way before us—lay it to heart, love it, read it, and learn what life is, what it means to be a man; aye, learn that God hath made us for himself, and unquiet are our hearts till they rest in Him. Make it your friend and teacher, and you will know what Sir Walter Scott meant when, as he lay dying, he asked Lockhart to read to him. "From what book?" asked Lockhart, and Scott replied, "There is but one Book!"

Chapter VI
RELIGION AND MASONRY

What does the word Religion mean? It is a Latin word of which there are two definitions, each pointing to a different side of the same thing. Cicero preferred the meaning "to think back," to recollect, to think over again, to reflect on the meaning of life. Others like best to define it as meaning "to rebind," to tie together, that which unites man to God and to his fellows. One thought runs through both definitions, the idea of a thread on which things are strung, a tie by which life is held together. It is not so much a separate faculty or interest, but a unity of all interests—an organizing principle among the values of life.

Take, for example, the life of Anton Tehekov of Russia. Something happened in him to kill all hope; some inner tragedy cut that tie that binds things together, scattering ideas and events everywhither, like beads when the thread is broken. It was no pose, but a real experience, and as bitter as real. He lost the sense of continuity, so that, as he said: "In all thoughts, feelings, and ideas which I form about anything there is wanting the Something Universal which could bind all these together into one whole." Events piled pell-mell without sequence or significance. Every man was merely himself, and had nothing in common with other men, like a tiny island in a lonely sea. No wonder he became a specialist in hopelessness, an artist of loneliness.

Religion, then, is that spiritual tie that binds us, first of all to God who is the "Something Universal" which unites all things into one whole; and second, to our fellow men in the service of duty and the fellowship of things immortal. It is that which organizes life, giving it unity, purpose and meaning, as over against an impulsive and unreflective existence. Truth, Love and "that thread of all-sustaining Beauty that runs through all and doth all unite," this is the eternal trinity; and in the deepest faith of humanity these three are one. From earliest time man has felt the tug of this threefold tie which unites him with God, with his fellow men, and with himself, linking his little life with the eternal enterprise. It is the spirit which gives coherence and cohesion to life, like the plan of a building and the cement which holds it together.

At once it will be seen that Masonry is one of the forms of the religious life, seeking to bind men together in faith, freedom, and friendship.

It is not a church, much less a sect, but it rests upon spiritual realities as the essential element in all true living, as well for the community as for the individual. It breaks the appalling loneliness in which men live, organizing them in spiritual faith, moral purpose, and eternal hope, holding them together by the cement of brotherly love and a common high endeavor. Indeed a Lodge, as has often been said, is a miniature prophecy of what Masonry would have the world become—a Beloved Community whose ordered life is made constructive by moral intelligence and practical good-will. Masonry knows that no brotherhood built on the baseness of human nature can long endure; it is a rope of sand. It toils in

> the dream, the wondrous dream
> Of a world without a seam!
> Man being one, as God is one,
> Brother's brother and Father's son,
> All earth, all Heaven, without a seam!

Other definitions, more picturesque, will make more vivid the meaning of Religion and Masonry. Three centuries ago there was born in Aberdeen, Scotland, a lad named Henry Scrougall, who entered the University at fifteen and was made Professor of Philosophy at the age of twenty. He died when twenty-eight, leaving only a tiny book to bear his name. It is a golden little book in which he tells us that "true religion is the union of the soul with God, the very image of God drawn in the soul—*the life of God in the soul of man.*" Because Religion is a Life, it can no more be shut up in a Church or a Lodge than spring can be confined in a garden; it takes all the forms that life and love and duty take.

The Teacher of Galilee did not use the word Religion at all, so far as we have record, but always the word Life instead. With him, whatever makes for deeper, purer, more fruitful life, is religious; whatever dwarfs, retards, or pollutes life is irreligious. With him religion did not consist in a few things to be done, but the spirit in which we do everything. To-day men are learning that religion is not a hierocratic mystery or a social convention, but a power, a faith by which to live the day through more deeply, more bravely, more joyously. All things have become religious that have in them the hope of joy and growth; all tasks are sacred which bring opportunity for fellowship; all things are from God which draw men together in good-will and promote justice and beauty in the earth. Religion is no longer a thing apart from life, but life itself at its highest and best—the life of God in the soul of man, which shakes the poison out of all our wild flowers.

One day in an old book-shop in London I found

a tiny book called *Psalms of the West,* by Rolla Russell. It was a book to love and live with, written out of a clear mind and a deep heart. He defines religion as "the union of the spirit of man with holiness, *the constant endeavor to do the best and bear the worst.*" It makes me think of the words of Emerson, who said that Religion is "the doing of all good, and for its sake the suffering of all evil." For we must suffer evil. Why it should be so no one knows, unless it is that by struggle we are to become strong and by suffering be made tender. Anyway, soon or late, in one form or another, the worst will befall each of us, leaving us prone upon the earth amid the ruin of our hopes. Only realities will sustain us then. When the blow falls, like the Master Builder in his dark, fatal hour, we can at least keep our moral integrity—though Death, or things worse than death, assail us with ruffian stroke.

Among the lovely spirits whom I met during my first summer in England, no one is more haunting than Donald Hankey, with whom I took tea in July before he was killed in October. He seems to stand before me now, slender, graceful, with a hesitating courtesy of address, as if reluctant to say farewell; a personality vivid and enchanting—the very memory of him is a footfall, always light, of one untimely gone away.

He summed up his faith in one line: *"Religion is just betting your life that there is a God."* It is a risk, an adventure, a faith. Literally, we live by faith every day, all the time. Otherwise, we should never cross a bridge, take a train, or make a friend. If a man acted only on what he knew, he would never move an inch. So, likewise, in the highest things, we must take risks, and it is always wise to trust the wisest and best. It appeals to the heroic in man, and Hankey was of the stuff of which heroes are made. He did not ask for advanced information that the battle is going to be a victory; he fought and won. He quoted to me the lines of Coleridge:

> "Think not the faith by which the just shall live
> Is a dead creed, a map correct of Heaven,
> Far less a feeling, fond and fugitive,
> A thoughtless gift, withdrawn as soon as given;
> It is an affirmation and an act
> That bids eternal truth be present fact."

When Thoreau lay on his last bed, and some one urged him to prepare for the world to come, he said, "One world at a time." That would be wise, if it were possible. But it is not. Man is a citizen of two worlds, and they are so interwoven that he cannot live in one at a time without ceasing to be a man. Religion, then, is *the art of living in two worlds at the same time,* each a fulfillment of the other. Busy himself as he may, seeking out many inventions, there are times when every man feels that old homesickness of the soul which has created all theologies. He knows, as his fathers knew before him, that he is a pilgrim and a stranger here, and he pauses to look away into the heavens. Were it otherwise, were man content with life as it is, then he would be no better than the beasts that perish. Then would the mountains be as a garden wall, the sea a mill pond, and the stars as the twinkling lights in a cottage window. Just when we are safest, and are about to be domesticated on earth, there is a touch of the Unseen, a voice from behind the hills of death, a quick impulse in the heart, and we know our destiny is elsewhere.

If I were asked to define religion, it would be to say that it is *the realization of the value of life*. Faith affirms that life has value, that, as Emerson said—thinking of his little boy long since fallen into dust—"what is excellent, as God lives, is permanent." Religion is the realization of the value of life both to ourselves and to God, and without that sense of value in life it loses its dignity. Moreover, if life is worthless, so is immortality, and all argument is useless. Once we realize the value of life we know that we are as immortal now as we shall ever be. To discover that fact, and live accordingly—laying our plans and forming our fellowships as citizens of eternity—is to be free from the things that hamper and dismay. This truth Masonry teaches with an overwhelming impressiveness, using the oldest, most heart-gripping drama in the world, not to tell us that there is a life beyond, but to initiate us into the eternal life here and now, showing us that *"religion is eternal life in the midst of time,* by the strength and under the eyes of God." Here is the great discovery, the great emancipation; and he who wins it is free indeed.

At least, in this informal way I hope I have made it plain that religion is a vital and living reality, and that Masonry is one of its myriad manifestations. The symbolism of our gentle Craft is simple, sublime, eloquent; it teaches the highest truth by the humblest emblems. Its whole genius is friendship, toleration, appreciation. It is not the enemy of any religion, but the friend of all influences toiling to build men up and to build them together, in the name of God and the spirit of fraternal goodness. Its whole purpose is to unite men, not to divide them; to join them in the quest of truth and the service of the moral ideal—blending a practical righteousness with the everlasting mercy. Its Lodges are centers of light in a dark world, where men of all races, ranks, parties and creeds meet in the name of a better humanity, a simple faith, a wiser justice, and a creative good-will.

Those great and simple words abide: "What doth the Lord require of thee but to do justly, to love mercy, and to walk humbly with thy God," words which Huxley held to be "as wonderful an inspiration of genius as the art of Phidias or the science of Aristotle." Let us join with them the words of the Apostle of Commonsense: "Pure and undefiled religion before God the Father is this: to visit the widows and orphans in their affliction, and to keep himself unspotted by the world." Here is the whole matter—the very genius of the Religion of Masonry: the upward look which links our fleeting mortal life with the spirit and will of God; the practical expression in fraternal service to our fellows in their sorrow and need; the inward integrity which realizes in character the supreme moral values. Reverence, benevolence, goodness—beyond that the profoundest thinker cannot go; short of that the simplest man need not stop. What more can the wisest sage tell us, what more can the best man do?

Chapter VII

THE BUILDERS [1]

"What mean ye by these stones?" By them we humbly affirm our faith in God as the Corner Stone and Master Builder of the Universe, knowing that they build in vain who build not on His foundations. Nothing can endure unless it is wrought in righteousness and good-will, in obedience to the Moral Law, in harmony with the creative and cohesive spirit of Love. Thus we seek to imitate on earth the wisdom and beauty of the Eternal Architect, His laws our rules, His rhythm our ritual.

"What mean ye by these stones?" By them we plight our faith in the Divinity of Man, his capacity for spiritual being, and the immutable necessity of fraternal righteousness as the cement of all society, more especially our own. We hold that to build a Beloved Community in freedom, friendship and moral worth is the purpose of the life of man which, by the worship of God

[1] Chant written for the laying of the Corner Stone of the great Masonic Temple of Detroit, Michigan, and reproduced here by the kindness of the Detroit *Masonic News*, Brother Douglas Martin, Editor.

and the service of humanity, we reverently seek to fulfill in the midst of the years.

"What mean ye by these stones?" By them we renew our allegiance to Home and Country and the House of God, pledging Freemasonry to the defense of Liberty, the practice of Justice, and the spread of Brotherly Love, Relief, and Truth, making the gains of industry upright, the use of power considerate, and the culture of good-will habitual; that Goodness may grow and be glorified and pity and joy walk the common ways of life.

"What mean ye by these stones?" By them we prophesy a time, or soon or late, when Love shall everywhere prevail, to the defeat of all unkindness and all uncleanness; when men of all creeds shall know that they love and seek one God, the Father of all; and folk of all races shall dwell together in mutual respect and good-will, in an unfortified world ruled by moral wisdom, spiritual intelligence, and practical fraternity. So mote it be.

PART TWO: *Practice*

Chapter VIII

PRACTICAL BROTHERHOOD

I

INDIVIDUAL BROTHERHOOD

"Alas, a Gospel of Brotherhood, not according to any of the Four old Evangelists, calling on men to amend each his own wicked existence, but a Gospel rather according to a new Fifth Evangelist, calling on men to amend each the whole world's wicked existence, and be saved by making a Constitution."—CARLYLE, "The French Revolution."

The world will never be better than the men who inhabit it. Everything begins and ends with the individual. One man living a Brotherly Life is worth a thousand lectures on Brotherhood. Men can make many things by wholesale, but great souls, faithful and generous hearts are made one by one. Commonplaces! it will be said. Even so. Bread, meat, sunlight, night and day are commonplace, but by such things men live. The trouble is that we fly so high that we overlook what is near by, building air-castles without foundation. Freemasonry is the realization of God and the practice of brotherhood, and it must begin with each of us in his own life.

Once for all the Great Brother of Galilee set forth this fact with unforgettable vividness in a story that one can read in two minutes. He told of "a certain man,"—it might be any man of any race—who went down from Jerusalem to Jericho, and was set upon by thieves who robbed him, beat him, and left him half dead. One can see the hard faces of the robbers silhouetted against the rocks—low-browed, dark-faced, with cruelty in their eyes—the plagues of society, desperadoes by calling, murderers by vocation.

There are the Priest and the Levite who journey that way, passing by the man in his distress. They are not hypocrites; they are simply men who separate religion from human service, as most men do. They tried to unite devotion to God with contempt of the need of mankind. They thought God lived in the Temple, listening to songs and prayers, not knowing that He is out on the highways of life where men faint and fall. It is the old atheism which divides piety from humanity, and thinks of religion as a sweet, dreamy emotion, rather than a matter of practical service.

There is the Samaritan—a heretic, an outcast, —with divine instincts, quick and keen sympathies, responsive to human need, asking no questions, but doing the thing that needed to be done. There is the innkeeper, kindly but business-like, glad to welcome the man who has been unfortunate, but glad also to have a paying guest, and happy to be assured that everything will be settled on business principles. It is an immortal picture of our human society, and in the living wisdom of the world there is nothing to surpass it alike in vividness and comprehensiveness.

The medicine for the sickness of the world, the way out of the blind alley into which it has run, the hope of a better day of justice and good-will, lies in the actual practice of brotherliness between man and man. Nothing can take the place of it. There is no substitute for it. No plan, no scheme, no program for a better world order is worth the paper it is written on, without men of the brotherly spirit. Whoso lives the brotherly life, however obscure he may be, does more for the world than all the orators. Professions of Brotherhood in a Masonic lodge are of no more value than professions of religion in a church—unless they are acted upon.

Such words need to be said again and again, each man to himself, if only to keep alive the sense of solemn and high responsibility in our own hearts. No one may shirk this matter, or shift it to another, without weakening the basis of society and making all holy things less secure. The Samaritan did not report the case of the man by the roadside to the Society for the Relief of the Distressed. He got down off his donkey, picked the man up, and took care of him. He did not denounce the Priest and Levite. He saw it as his duty, did it, and went on about his business.

But let us go a little further. Some one has said that it is easier to give five dollars to a beggar than it is to forgive a man who rides his logic ruthlessly over our pet prejudices. It is easier to help a man who is down—whether by his own folly or the fault of another—than to give a square deal to one who is in the race with us for the prizes of life. Philanthropy is one thing; justice is another. In time of dire need men want charity; justice they want all the time. The ancient prophet had the true order of things when he told us what is required of us: "To do justly, to love mercy, and to walk humbly with thy God." Here is the idea in a very striking, searching poem by Ina Coolbirth:

> "O Soul! however sweet
> The goal to which I hasten with swift feet—
> If, just within my grasp,
> I reach, and joy to clasp,

And find there one whose body I must make
    A footstool for that sake,
Though ever and for evermore denied,
    Grant me to turn aside!"

II

ORGANIZED BROTHERHOOD

"The principal intention of forming societies is undoubtedly the uniting men in the stricter bands of love; for men, considered as social creatures, must derive their happiness from each other; every man being designed by Providence to promote the good of others, as he tenders his own advantage; and by that intercourse to secure their good offices, by being, as occasion may offer, serviceable to them."—CHARLES BROCKWELL, "A Charge to Masons," 1749.

Masonry is organized brotherhood. Because fellowship is a source both of joy and of power, because we can do together what we could never do alone, men are drawn together and joined together in a great fraternity, the better to promote the principle and practice of brotherhood in their own lives and in the life of the world. Such an order of men, ancient, universal, beneficent—made up of select men trained and sworn to help make righteousness prevail—is a prophecy of that spirit, that tendency, that tie which at last

    "Shall bind each heart and nation
      In one grand brotherhood of men
    And one high consecration."

Masonic philanthropy is an honor and an ornament to the Craft. It does the work of the Good Samaritan, taking care of the widow, the orphan, the aged and infirm with a munificence as beautiful as it is gracious. Besides, in ways innumerable and untraceable the spirit of Masonry mitigates the hard lot of many outside the order. Only the art of an angel could record the ways in which Masons help one another, showing a brotherliness truly practical in sickness and in difficulty. Wrought in secret, under cover of Masonic silence, only a tiny part of this untiring ministry is known to the world—and that is as it should be.

Unfortunately the thieves who robbed the man on the road to Jericho escaped. Nothing more is said about them in the parable. No doubt they robbed other travelers. Here is one of the dark problems of the world, weaving a shadowy fringe on the borders of human society. The Good Samaritan did not remove the cause of the misery he helped to heal. He could not do it alone. Hence the necessity of organized fraternity, that together we may clean out the den of thieves, and make the highways of the world safe for all who travel on lawful avocations. The State, in any great conception of it, is an organized brotherhood, and Masonry labors unceasingly to inculcate that idea. An unworthy citizen cannot be a good Mason.

Masonry is organized patriotism. Neither a political party nor a religious sect, it none the less stands for just laws and the spirit of loyalty and coöperation without which the State cannot be stable and effective. Patriotism is the translation of private faith and individual righteousness into terms of public virtue and social service. Nothing less than this is worthy of the name. The crying need of to-day is to extend the spirit and principles of Masonry to the whole life and transactions of mankind—and this must begin by extending them to all the transactions of Masons. The failure to do this accounts for the deficit between private morality and public morality. Men as a group, as a party, as a corporation will do what not one of them would do as an individual. The responsibility is distributed until it evaporates; and so we have a public and corporate life which is a reproach to the character of the community. When we are truly patriotic this will not be so.

Practical brotherhood, if it has any meaning at all, means that all men, regardless of race, rank, or creed, shall have an opportunity to live and to live well—that even the humblest child, to the measure of its capacity, shall be admitted to the full inheritance of humanity. It will not merely be friendly to, but will help forward every wise effort in behalf of a full, free, happy, useful life for all classes, and will seek to organize civilization to that end. Masonry, in its organized capacity, may not formulate or support definite political and social programs; but it will create and cultivate in its members the will and the passion to be champions of every cause which endeavors intelligently to build a better human order.

III

APPLIED BROTHERHOOD

"We are all blind until we see
That in the human plan
Nothing is worth the making if
It does not make the man.

Why build these cities glorious
If man unbuilded goes?
In vain we build the work unless
The builder also grows."
—Edwin Markham.

That is to say, Masonry is the application of noble ideas to practical life. If it merely ends in fine emotion or eloquent sentiment, it fails. Ideas do not work themselves out automatically. Some seem to think that all we have to do is to throw a great idea into the world, and then by virtue of some magic power that truth possesses, it will begin to work and bear fruit of its own accord. It is not so. There must be soil for the seed, and hard work in its cultivation. Ideas by themselves are ghosts until they are incarnated in men, and the men are organized for the service of the truth.

Great ideas are simple enough, but their application is complex and difficult. For example, many men to-day—men who are in no sense Socialists—refuse to accept the present industrial order as final. It makes money, but it mutilates humanity. Commercially it may be a triumph, but humanly it is sadly imperfect, and its injustice is only equaled by its ugliness. We cannot see the next step, but there must be a way to bring back beauty and joy into the work of the world, which is now so often a drudgery and a grind. Ruskin was right when he said that life without industry is sin, and industry without beauty is brutality. He was also right when he wrote:

"There is no wealth but life—life, including all its powers of love, of joy, of admiration. That country is richest which nourishes the greatest number of noble and happy human beings; that man is richest who, having perfected the functions of his own life to the utmost, has also the widest influence, both personal, and by means of his possessions, over the lives of others."

Our ancient Operative Brethren came nearer solving these vexing questions than any one has ever come since. They worked as a fraternity; they had joy in their work, and saw spiritual meaning in it. Labor was a joy to them because it was constructive, and because they never lost the human touch—which is the saddest tragedy of modern industry. Their labor was communal. Each man worked as a brother in a community, not as a cog in a machine. It was mixed with friendliness, comradeship, and good-will. They regarded their ingenuity—both as artists and as artisans—as a form of divine inspiration, a holy and consecrated skill, for which they gave thanks as a community on Whit-Sunday. The Master was not a Foreman or an Overseer; he was a Brother, a friend, a teacher.

Surely modern industry is not the better for the loss of this spirit of reverence and coöperation—brotherly leadership and communal responsibility—which distinguished the fraternity of Operative Freemasonry. To-day Master and Man are far apart. They have little personal contact. Social welfare work in factories is too much like a sop to the discontented—too much like a form of charity. Men go to their work

PRACTICAL BROTHERHOOD

as if driven, finding no joy in it, shirking it as much as possible. Our ancient Brethren never thought of getting all they could for as little work as possible. The whole idea of using men to make money, instead of using money to make men, is foreign to the genius and history of Masonry. No Mason was regarded as a "hand"; he was a fellow, a brother—not an animated tool but a human being. There is no hope of peace in the industrial world until this spirit of humanity and fraternity is recovered—restoring the status of labor, and also its high obligation. Masonry did it once; Masonry can help to do it again.

Masonry is an international fraternity. Its members are prepared to travel in foreign countries and work and receive the wages of a Master Mason. Each is enjoined to be loyal to his own country, without hatred of other lands—knowing that other men love their countries as he loves his. In all the teaching of Masonry there is a recognition of the human race as a family, a brotherhood—a sense of the fact that the good of humanity as a whole does actually exist—and that is the one thing needed to day. The world is perishing for lack of Brotherhood, and though we have the great ideal on our lips, it has not yet found its way into our hearts and hands.

"Does it make you mad when you read about
Some poor, starved devil who flickered out,
Because he had never a decent chance
In the tangled meshes of circumstance?
If it makes you burn like the fires of sin,
Brother, you are fit for the ranks—fall in!

Does it makes you rage when you come to learn
Of a clean-souled woman who could not earn
Enough to live, and who fought, but fell
In the cruel struggle and went to hell?
Does it make you seethe with an anger hot?
Brother, we welcome you—share our lot!

Whoever has blood that will flood his face
At the sight of Beast in the holy place;
Whoever has rage for the tyrant's might,
For the powers that prey in the day and night,
Whoever has hate for the ravening Brute
That strips the tree of its goodly fruit;
Whoever knows wrath at the sight of pain,
Of needless sorrow and heedless gain;

Whoever knows bitterness, shame and gall
At thought of the trampled ones doomed to fall;
He is a brother-in-soul, we know;
With brain afire and with soul aglow;
By the sight of his eyes we sense our kin—
Brother, you battle with us—fall in!"

Chapter IX

THE DOCTRINE OF THE BALANCE

Readers of Albert Pike will recall the stately pages with which *Morals and Dogma* closes, setting forth, in a manner unforgettable, the Doctrine of the Balance. Many had taught this truth before time out of mind, no one more impressively than the man to whom Pike was richly indebted,[1] but his exposition is none the less his own. With vast labor he brings together his findings, showing that to this result the wisdom of the ages runs, what the sages have thought equally with what the mystics have dreamed. Always it is a triad, suggested by the ancient idea of the number Three, the singular, the dual and the plural, the odd and even added, and the great emblem of the Triangle—symbol of perfection. It is seen in all Masonic symbolism, from end to end and at every step of the mystic quest for the secret which every Mason is seeking.

Eloquently, and with every variation of emphasis and illustration, he lays the matter before us, carrying it into all the fields of human ac-

---

[1] Eliphas Levi. "Digest of His Writings," translated by A. E. Waite, especially pp. 79-83.

tivity and aspiration. Sympathy and Antipathy, Attraction and Repulsion, Fate and Freedom, each a fact of life and a force of nature, are contraries alike in the universe and in the soul of man, wherein we see eternity in miniature. As the earth is held in its orbit by the action of opposing forces, so truth is made up of two opposite propositions, as peace lies in the union of motion and rest, and harmony is the fruit of seeming war. Here he finds the solution of the problem of the One and the Many, of the Infinite and the Finite, of Unity amidst Manifoldness: the principle of the Balance, the secret of the universal equilibrium:

"Of that Equilibrium in the Deity, between the Infinite Divine Wisdom and the Infinite Divine Power, from which result the Stability of the Universe, the unchangeableness of the Divine Law, and the Principles of Truth, Justice, and Right which are a part of it; . . . Of that Equilibrium also, between the Infinite Divine Justice and the Infinite Divine Mercy, the result of which is the Infinite Divine Equity, and the Moral Harmony or Beauty of the Universe. By it the endurance of created and imperfect natures in the presence of a Perfect Deity is made possible; . . .

"Of that Equilibrium between Necessity and Liberty, between the action of the Divine Omnipotence and the Free-will of man, by which vices and base actions, and ungenerous thoughts and words are crimes and wrongs, justly punished by the law of cause and consequence, though nothing in the universe can happen or be done contrary to the will of God; and without which coexistence of Liberty and Necessity, of Free-will in the creature and Omnipotence in the Creator, there could be no religion, nor any law of right and wrong, or merit or demerit, nor any justice in human punishments or penal laws. . . .

"And, finally, of that Equilibrium, possible in ourselves, and which Masonry incessantly labors to accomplish in its Initiates and demands of its Adepts and Princes (else unworthy of their titles), between the Spiritual and Divine and the Material and Human in man; between the Intellect, Reason, and Moral Sense on one side, and the Appetites and Passions on the other, from which result the Harmony and Beauty of a well-regulated life." [2]

And so on, through a passage of singular elevation both of language and of thought, we are led by an ancient truth which becomes a vision in the mind of a nobler thinker. My design is not to add to his exposition, but to apply it with emphasis and illustration, if so that it may be brought home to our "business and bosom" and be of real service to us in the life which we live together, and in the life which each must live alone. For it is the high service of Masonry that it puts a man in the straight path which the wisest of the race have walked, leading him midway between the falsehood of extremes, and

[2] "Morals and Dogma," pp. 859-60.

bringing the highest teaching of the past to the uses of the present. After all, how to live is the one matter; and he is wise who joins the goodly Shakespeare gospel of Courage, Sanity and Pity with that other Gospel of Faith, Hope, and Love. Every man will need all the aid he can get, unless he be content, as no real man can be, to live in the world as a mere looker-on at a drama in which others are actors—

> "In God's vast house a curious guest,
> Seeing how all works take their flight."

From bottom to top life is a contradiction and a paradox, and the beginning of wisdom is to know that fact and adjust ourselves to it. Light and darkness, heat and cold, mind and matter, fate and free-will, asceticism and indulgence, socialism and anarchy, dogmatism and doubt, reason and authority—no man may ever hope to live long enough, much less to think deeply enough, to harmonize these paradoxes. The way of wisdom is to accept both facts in each case, as the Two Pillars of a Temple of Truth, and walk between them into the hush of the holy place. Either one, without the other, is only a half-truth which ends in perversion, if not in insanity, turning the hearty, wholesome, clear-seeing spirit of manhood into the pitiful narrowness and hardness of a bigot or a fanatic.

THE DOCTRINE OF THE BALANCE 101

For example: "All is free—that is false: all is fate—that is false. All things are free and fated—that is true." [3] It is possible to make an argument in behalf of fatalism so freezing that one is left with the feeling that he is no more responsible for his thoughts and acts, than he is for the shape of his head and the color of his eyes. Having listened to such argument, each of us may say, as Dr. Johnson did,[4] "I know I am free, and that's the end on it." On the other side, one can present a thesis in proof of the freedom of man so convincing that fate seems a fiction. Both are true, and the great truth consists of two opposites which are not contradictory—that it is the Fate of man to be Free if he fights for it, approves himself worthy of it, uniting his will with the Will of the Master of the World! Otherwise, we men are slaves journeying downward "to the dust of graves," slaves of greed and passion and a fatal folly.

Asceticism is one extreme, indulgence another. One would repress every natural instinct in behalf of a pale, wan purity; the other would follow every fancy, driven hither and yon by every gust of passion, at the mercy of every caprice. Between the two lies temperance, keeping the balance between two absurdities, making a right use

[3] "Life of F. W. Robertson," p. 32, note.
[4] "Life of Johnson," by Boswell.

of everything, and abusing nothing; its motto the wise words of the old Greeks, "In nothing too much." Socialism seems to hold that the State is everything, the Individual nothing—or at best only a cog in a vast machine, an atom in an indistinguishable blur. Anarchy makes the State nothing, and the Individual everything—each a law unto himself, and chaos at the end. Between the two lies the way of wise government in which "Freedom slowly broadens down from precedent to precedent," or grows gladly up from the life of a just and intelligent people. There are certain things which every man must surrender in behalf of the common good, and other things which it were a sin to abdicate, the while a shifting, zig-zag line runs between dividing the man from the mass.

By the same token, in religion Dogmatism affirms everything, makes a map of the Infinite, and an atlas of Eternity, so certain is it of things whereof no man knoweth. It talks of God as if He were a man in the next room. It knows the origin of all things, and the final destiny of humanity. Doubt denies everything, questions the competence of the human mind to know Divine things, leaving us with the assurance that nothing is certain but uncertainty; nothing secure but insecurity. Again it is the doctrine of the balance, as in the natural world peace is found amid

THE DOCTRINE OF THE BALANCE

the poise of powers. Between dogmatism and doubt is a wise and reverent Faith, which dares to say, "Now we know in part—a tiny part, no doubt—but knowledge is real as far as it goes, and what we know gives us confidence in the vast Unknown. And so we make bold to trust the ultimate decency of things and the veiled kindness of the Father of men, assured that He who has brought us to where we are will lead us to where we ought to be!"

Of this fundamental paradox of life the Cross is the symbol. Older than Christianity,—as old, almost, as human life,—it is the supreme symbol of the race. When man first emerged from the "old dark backward and abysm of time," he had a cross in his hand. Where he got it, what he meant by it, many may conjecture but no one knows. The Cross, like life itself, is also a collision and a contradiction—its four arms pointing everywhither, making it the great guide-post of free thought. As long as a man keeps his poise, never forgetting the profound paradox at the heart of all high thought, he may think as far and as fast as his mind can go. For many of us, of course, the Cross is hallowed anew and forever by the name of One whose life was a tragedy, whose love was heroic in its gentleness, who wins by "that strange power called weakness," whose character is the sovereign wonder of the world, and whose spirit is the holiest tradition of humanity.

Since this is so, since the way of sanity, if not of salvation, lies in keeping our balance, why is it that men lose their poise? No man of us, when he thinks of the days agone, but recalls acts which he not only regrets, but which puzzle him by their strange stupidity. He would give almost as much to be able to understand them as he would to forget them. Why is this so? Shakespeare has much to teach us here, much of abiding profit to remember, if so that we may understand the past and make a better use of the future. He everywhere shows that tragedy is the fruit of treachery, and that treachery has its roots in obsession [5]—some one thing that gets so close to the mind that it can see nothing else, blinds it, preys upon it, making a man first a fanatic, and then, it may be, a criminal. Macbeth was a man of noble nature; his wife was a lovely lady. They became obsessed with ambition for place and power, and to what dark depths of sin and shame that mad blindness led them that terrible tragedy tells us. This lesson, taught so often by our supreme poet, is for each of us, teaching us to keep our poise, and to flee an obsession as a plague. Whatever fastens itself upon the mind, shutting out the light, marring

---

[5] "Shakespeare," by John Masefield.

the proportions and perspectives of things, forebodes disaster.

Perhaps it is physical passion. If so, it will turn love into lust and make the world a bawdyhouse. It may be political ambition, and a man throws everything to the winds in order to win, forgetting that no office on earth is worth the sacrifice of integrity—and, also, if he wins by trickery he is unfit to hold it. It may be religion. Think of the crimes unspeakable, the brutalities unbelievable, which have been committed by men in a frenzy of fanatical bigotry—dipping their hands in blood and thinking they were doing the will of God! They were madmen. Plato said that all men are more or less insane, and that the man whom we put in a strait-jacket is only a little more emphatically out of his mind than the rest of us. The more reason, then, why we should keep our poise and walk the quiet way of sanity and charity, in love of God and man.

After this manner we expound the Doctrine of the Balance, as taught by Pike, reminding our Brethren, as we remind ourselves, that the wisdom of life lies in freedom, serenity, and forgiveness, in victory by self-surrender to the highest laws of life, and that we dare not turn either to the right or the left. By such teaching men become happy and free; in this way we may grow old without being sad, and wise without being cynical; and learn, at last, that everlasting gentleness which is the highest wisdom man may win from the hard facts and the often strange medley of his days. Let us also lay to heart the prayer quoted by Pike:

"Let Him, the ever-living God, be always present in thy mind; for thy mind itself is His likeness, for it, too, is invisible and impalpable, and without form. As He exists forever, so thou also, when thou shalt put off this which is visible and corruptible, shalt stand before Him forever, living and endowed with knowledge."

Chapter X

THE MASTER

Hear now the history of a word as it has come down to us from days of old. In the ancient Guilds of artisans, the skilled metalsmiths of the Middle Ages, an Apprentice toiled for seven years at his tasks. When at last his hand was trained, and he had wrought some beautiful thing, perhaps in beaten silver, he brought it to the Master of the Guild and said, "Behold my experience!" Having worked for seven long years, the sum of all his impassioned patience and aspiration was in that tiny bit of shining metal; it was a symbol of his character which, as the word tells us, is something carved.

Like every man who achieves a delicate and difficult task, he had made many mistakes, had spoiled many a piece of metal, had dulled the edge of many a tool. He had spent painful days and nights in labor, and his Masterpiece, his Experience, was the sum and reward of all his Experiments. He had given himself to his task with enthusiasm; he had obeyed his Master; his faith had made him faithful—and the whole was in that tiny bit of silver. He might now take his kit of tools and go out as a journeyman, a Master of his Craft.

Which story is a parable of how a man becomes a Master Mason, not by receiving a Degree, but by the attainment of a habitual mastery of his appetites and passions by the Reason and the Moral Sense; a habitual mastery, as Pike reminds us, not a never-failing mastery—for that is a trophy which few mortals win in this world. The task of every man is to take the raw material of his life, with whatever of glowing passion or hard heredity it may hold; take it as it is, and by patience in spite of blunders, by perseverance in face of failures, by loyalty to an Ideal and fidelity to a noble Life-plan, shape it into a constant beauty and enduring worth.

No man who has tried it needs to be told that this is no easy task, albeit for some it is easier than for others—it was easier for Emerson than for Burns, who tried so hard and failed so much. By the same token, since every man fights a hard fight, no one can boast over his fellow; and if, by reason of rare power or a sweeter ancestry he is unhampered by the failures of his fathers, it is the more reason why he should be an inspiration and aid to his fellow men. No man wins this victory all at once, or once for all. Let him who thinketh he standeth take heed lest he fall, for the enemies of Mansoul are many and exceeding cunning.

As Huxley said, "It does not take much of a man to be a Christian, but it takes all there is of him," and he might have added that it takes all his time. Just so, if one would be a Master Mason in very truth, and not in name only or the wearing of a pin, he will find that it asks for all that he has of wisdom and of wit, the while he divides his time into labor, rest, and the service of his kind. How well Wordsworth knew when he wrote:

> " 'Tis the most difficult of tasks to keep
> Heights which the soul is competent to gain:
> Man is of dust;"

and as all are made of the selfsame dust, it becomes us to be gentle as it behooves us to be just. More and more, as we grow older, and learn the perils of the road, and remember how often we have failed and how far we have wandered, the words of Goethe come to mind:

"If during our lifetime we see that performed by others to which we ourselves felt an earlier call, but had been obliged to give up, with much besides, then the beautiful feeling enters the mind, that only mankind together is the true man, and that the individual can only be joyous and happy when he has the courage to feel himself in the whole."

Here is the great Fraternity in whose heroic and inspiring fellowship we live, and by whose inspiration we may win victory—man in God, and God in Man willing the God to be! Yet in each soul there is something unique, something not to be found anywhere else, a beauty peculiar, particular, precious, as no two leaves on a tree are alike, and no two sunsets the same. Each man must make Research to find that hidden Pearl of Eternity within his own soul; that star which shines for him alone—"My Star," as Browning called it; and having found it, let him follow it and he will find himself, his Brother, and his God. Even so, each of us, by mastery of himself, may add a pearl of great price to the common wealth; each may set a new star in that sky which arches over our human world.

> "Oh! the cedars of Lebanon grow at our door,
>   And the quarry is sunk at our gate;
> And the ships out of Ophir, with golden ore,
>   For our summoning mandate wait;
> And the word of a Master Mason
>   May the house of our soul create!
> While the day hath light let the light be used,
>   For no man shall the night control!
> Or ever the silver cord be loosed,
>   Or broken the golden bowl,
> May we build King Solomon's Temple
>   In the true Masonic soul!"

What though a man win wealth and the applause of fame, and have not Charity, it is nothing; what though he sway the world with his eloquence and miss the high prize of "self-knowledge, self-reverence and self-control," even if men erect an obelisk of gold above his grave it is a monument to a failure. He only is wise who lives a simple, sincere, faithful life, building on the Square by the Plumb, toiling in the light of Eternity; as Browning would say, did we alter one word in his lines—

> "Masonry is all or nothing; it's no mere smile
> Of contentment, sigh of aspiration, sir—
> No quality of the finelier tempered clay
> Like its whiteness or its lightness; rather, stuff
> Of the very stuff; life of life, and self of self."

Chapter XI

KNIGHTS OF A NEW CRUSADE

It is curious how interpreters of history disagree in their reading of the days when knighthood was in flower. Freeman holds that the virtues of chivalry were unreal and its program fantastic, while Burke is equally sure that it was at once picturesque and noble, the unbought grace of civilization and the cheap defense of nations. No doubt, if we take the history of knighthood as a whole, much might be said on both sides—since good and ill are mixed in all things human—but he is a poor historian, and no poet at all, who does not see that the good far outweighed and out-topped the bad.

Anyway, in all history it would be hard to find a chapter more thrilling, more multi-colored and romantic, alike in its organization and achievement, than the story of the Knightly Orders, from the legends of King Arthur and the Knights of the Round Table to the days when Cervantes made a movement which had served its purpose ridiculous. Who that has read the legends of Winchester, or *The Talisman,* by Sir Walter

Scott, to name no others, has not felt his heart beat fast in response to the gallant idealism, the poetic militant love, the daring courage, the long quests, the mystical faith of the old knighthood, with its grace and charm of courtesy, its lighthearted valor, its genius of gentleness, its spirit of disinterested service! Whatever may have been its later perversions and corruptions, at its best there was something high and fine, heroic and winsome, in the story of the Knights of the Holy Cross.

At this distance the story of the Crusades reads like a legend, in the goal they set out to reach no less than in the enthusiasm by which they were inspired. Suddenly, by a mysterious religious impulse, the West seemed to turn Eastward, moving in mass to rescue the Holy Land from the hand of the Saracens and to restore the sacred places. The military order of the Templars was founded in 1119 to protect the roads and defend the pilgrims to the Holy Land. They took vows of poverty, chastity and obedience, and were given quarters in Jerusalem on the site of the Temple, from which they derived their name. The Holy Land was under the dominion of the Turk—then, as now, an enemy of Christian civilization—and the pilgrim had not only to submit to heavy taxation and pillage when he arrived, but had to encounter perils of brigands on the road—passing many graves along the way. There was also the danger of disease, and the Knights Hospitalers were reorganized and granted a charter by Godfrey de Bouillon for medical and ambulance work.

Thus protection was joined with relief; but after the enthusiasm of the Crusades waned, both orders grew wealthy, fell from their high purpose, and were in course of time expelled from Palestine. Their work done, the Knights Templars retired to the fertile lands of central Europe, and lived in luxury, with nothing to justify their existence. Not unnaturally their wealth excited the greed of Philip of France, who directed his tool, Pope Clement V., to summon the Grand Master of the Order, Jacques de Molay, to appear before him. When he appeared, with one hundred and forty Templars, he was seized and thrown into prison, where he was put to death. The Order was suppressed in 1312, having been charged with the blackest crimes—after the manner of the time and at the behest of envy and greed—its property confiscated, and its labors brought to an end.

Just how the Order of the Templars survived in the form of Christian Masonry is a story wrapped in obscurity. One theory holds that De Molay appointed a successor, and that there has been an unbroken line of Grand Masters of the

Order since his martyrdom. Others assert that the Chevalier Ramsey created a Masonic order of Knights Templar in aid of the exiled Stuarts; but neither theory seems to be capable of proof —though that does not mean that the first theory may not be true, since, in the history of a secret and persecuted order, much is true which, in the nature of things, cannot be proved by dates and documents. This at least is true; it was in accord with the fitness of things that Masonry and Christianity should in some way be joined, and a fine poetic insight wrought that union by reviving, or perpetuating, the symbolism, the romance, the high and gallant spirit of the ancient Order of the Temple, and making it the Christian form of Freemasonry. This is also true: Nothing in the ceremonies of Masonry is more stately or impressive than the degrees of Chivalric Masonry; and no man with eyes to see and a heart to understand can yield himself to their beauty and truth without being made a nobler, gentler, more Christ-like man. What the Square is in the Craft, the Cross is in the Order of the Temple.

So much for the past. No doubt there was something quixotic and futile, much of madness and superstition, as well as many cruelties and barbarities, in the old Crusades; but these were no essential part of the crusade idea. Every crusade has three elements: First, a definite goal, rising luminous and alluring before the mind, bewitching men with passion and power. Second, a passionate enthusiasm which burns all lesser ambitions, all evil desires, and which reckons no sacrifice too great to attain the goal. Third, a loyalty to one Supreme Commander so intense that all are melted into one solid phalanx and sent against the foe. Has Christian Masonry to-day these elements by which it may be counted worthy of the great succession in which it stands? Has it a definite goal, a passionate enthusiasm, and an all-transfiguring loyalty to the Commander—Captain of all the forces of gentleness and goodness among men—whose Cross is its symbol and its banner? In short, does Christian Masonry justify its existence in a manner worthy of its history and its genius? Should there not be a new Crusade in our day?

If you ask what shall be the goal of a New Crusade, my reply is, the rescue of America and its leadership in the service of humanity —the making of a better social order and the winning of a warless world! Is not that a goal worthy of the ambition of a new crusade, an adventure asking for a gallant and holy chivalry worthy of the new order of the ages? All the foes that wrecked the old civilizations are organized and active to-day. The Saracen of the twelfth century has gone, but the Saracen of the twentieth century is here, insolent and defiant, infesting the roads to a freer and better social order—a bandit and a brigand. Who is he? He is the materialist, the cynic, the sensualist, the unscrupulous politician, the dishonest merchant, the bigot who breeds bitterness, the greedy capitalist, the anarchistic wage-earner, the law breaker, the law hater, the man who works iniquity and makes a lie in the holy places of life. There is a spirit among us, vigilant, alert, aggressive, and wholly hostile to the higher human life. Whether it take the form of mercenary greed, egoistic vanity, lust of power, or religious bigotry, it is the same, and it never sleeps. Its wits are quickened by every motive of gain, its resources are as manifold as the genius of avarice can invent, and its courage is the boldness of selfishness guided by guile.

America is in danger: he is blind who does not see it. America may yet be lost: he who doubts it has never put his ear to the ground and heard the roar of the subterranean fires which seethe and hiss under the thin crust of our civilization. Long ago Lowell said, "Democracy is only an experiment," and the experiment is not yet completed. Without spiritual leadership, without moral idealism, without practical fraternity, democracy fails. The land of Washington and Lincoln is our Holy Land, and we dare not let it be overrun by ruthless selfishness and greed, by narrow fanaticism and blind stupidity. To beat back the Saracen, to rescue America from materialism, lawlessness and irreligion, to recover the old tradition of simple faith and faithful service to a land dedicated to liberty, fraternity and God, making it an instrument in His hand for the redemption of civilization from the suicide of war—here is a crusade worthy of the finest chivalry of Christian Masonry!

Two swords are in our hands—two swords that flash and glitter in the sunlight—noble private character and an intelligent, organized, and articulate public-mindedness. Character is the first and fundamental thing. It is at once the cornerstone and the keystone of society and the state, the basis of an ordered and stable civilization. When all is said, the best service any man can render to his race is the building of a noble, refined, heroic moral character. Such men are in very truth the salt of the earth, without which the whole human fabric rots and falls to pieces. Here our gentle and wise Freemasonry—being a society of men seeking goodness—helps to make all holy things more radiant, all divine things more real. In the spirit of fellowship, without hasting and without resting, it toils in behalf of such righteousness as King David set to music in his description of the Religion of a Gentleman, in the 15th Psalm. Let us humbly thank God for an Order, so widespread over the earth, whose emphasis upon the practice of righteousness is never relaxed, and whose influence in the making of good men no man can measure.

But character must be organized and find expression in the making of an intelligent and moral public-mindedness. The knights of old were great gentlemen—men of high and chivalrous character—but in order to fight the Saracen they had to unite, taking vows of purity, service and sacrifice. So we must help to organize the moral intelligence of America, if we are to meet the enemies which threaten our Republic and keep its holy places inviolate. Our spiritual-mindedness must be made practically effective in an intelligent and articulate public-mindedness. One reads a scientific study of *Public Opinion,* by Walter Lippmann, with a sense of dismay, realizing how much we lack the high disinterestedness so vital to our welfare. Ignorance, indifference, and stupid selfishness—these are the foes against which we fight, and in this war there can be no truce.

Here is the challenge to a new knighthood—new in its armor, but fighting with the old chivalry, generosity, and courtesy—calling us to make war with the Sword of the Spirit, with a courage as bright and an intelligence as keen as that of the white knights of olden time. Against all uncleanness, all unkindness, all bigotry and brutality, in defense of the weak, in championship of the oppressed, we make war in the name of Him whose Cross is our symbol, to whom we offer our prayer—like the heroic and merciful knight in the brave days agone:

> "Keep, in Thy pierced hands
>   Still the bruised helmet;
> Let not their hostile bands
>   Wholly o'erwhelm it!
> Bless my poor shield for me,
>   Christ, King of Chivalry.
> Keep Thou my sullied mail,
>   Lord, that I tender
> Here, at Thine altar-rail!
>   Then—let Thy splendor
> Touch it once—and I go
>   Stainless to meet the foe!"

Chapter XII

MASONRY IN AMERICAN HISTORY

Lord Charnwood said recently that the history of America, if told with insight and imagination, is one of the greatest epics of the world. It is true. No tale of fairyland is more romantic than the story of the discovery and development of America. Because it is familiar to us—if, indeed, it is familiar—we do not realize how thrilling was the settlement and conquest of a continent in the face of untamed nature and savage human nature. For America is not a new England. It is not a new Europe. It is a New World, in which are to be wrought out the highest ideals of the race in its long quest of fraternal righteousness.

Never, since time began, has there been such a flowing together of peoples, such a blending of bloods, such a unity evolved from diversity. The Pilgrims and Puritans of New England, stern, heroic, God-fearing, liberty-loving; the Dutch of New Amsterdam, sturdy, thrifty, wholesome; the blessed Quakers of Jersey, whose tradition of sweetness and earnestness is a precious legacy;

the men of the Old Dominion and the Carolinas —these laid the foundations of a new society in a New World. Others came later, Germans following successive waves of revolution at home, the Irish with their wit and charm and sagacity, peoples many from lands many, crossing mountain, plain and prairie, as their fathers crossed the sea; making a path where no path was; until, to-day, if from some sky-ship we could look down upon the whole scene, what a picture it would be—rivers like threads of silver, cities shining in the sunlight, railways moving like shuttles in a loom, park-like farms dotted with happy homes—all built with amazing rapidity on a continent unencumbered by institutions of earlier races, where freedom could grow and be glorified.

No one race, no one influence made America. It is a composite, a symposium, a fraternal enterprise and achievement, in which many races and many forces have mingled, all working, under God, toward one Divine intent. Surely he is a poor patriot, and no poet at all, who, looking back over the story of our country, does not see in it the shaping hand of the Eternal Good-will, and hear the footsteps of a beneficent Destiny. Time and again, in hours of crisis and confusion, we have seen things turn, unaccountably, as if touched by a Hand put forth from the Unseen, directing us in the way appointed by the Lord of History. In every hour of tragedy and desperate demand, a man has stepped forth from the shadow to match the mortal need—a man of providential personality, providentially trained for his task—Washington in the hour of Revolution, Lincoln in a day of Rebellion, Roosevelt in a time when Materialism seemed triumphant, Wilson in the stupendous moment of universal calamity. America has nothing to fear save the decay of manhood, the betrayal of its own principles, the rot of luxury, and the denial of that grand moral idealism which has been the creative impulse of its history, and which, so far, with whatever variation, has been true, in the end, to its genius and its prophecy.

To be more specific, and tracing one thread woven into the fabric of moral, spiritual, and social history, let us think for a moment of the influence of Freemasonry in the story of America. Gentle, silent, ever-present, always active, unhasting, unresting, by its constructive genius our Fraternity has built itself into the foundation and superstructure of this Republic. Only the pen of some great Angel, moved by some unearthly skill, could tell the real history of Masonry in America. Such a theme belongs of right to poetry and song, or else to some art delicate enough to record the biography of a fragrance or the memoirs of a sentiment. Yet, as history has more than once made plain, it is just these imponderable, intangible forces which mold the destiny of nations, as of individuals, making the very air they breathe, and touching with intellectual and spiritual fineness their enterprise and aspiration. Who could measure the influence, much less estimate the worth, of all the Masonic altars in this land, where men meet in the name of God and the moral law, seeking that truth which makes us men and that spiritual character which gives to law its authority and to society its refinement and its stability!

Masonry came early to America. Long before the name "United States" had ever been uttered, our gentle Craft was busy among the builders of the New World, and it must be reckoned among the powers making for righteousness all down our history. Along the Atlantic coast, among the Great Lakes, in the wilderness of the Middle West, in the far South, everywhere in centers of population and in little Upper Rooms on the frontier, we see the Lodge alongside the Home, the Church and the School. When our fathers asserted that "governments derive their just powers from the consent of the governed," Masonry was present at the birth of our Republic, with whose history it has had so much to do. No one need be told what patriotic memories cluster about the old Green Dragon Tavern in Boston, which Webster called "the headquarters of the Revolution," and it was also the headquarters of Freemasonry in the old Bay State, where the Boston Tea Party was planned. As in Massachusetts, so throughout the Colonies, Masonry was everywhere active, indirectly as an order, but directly through its members, in behalf of a nation "conceived in liberty and dedicated to the proposition that all men are created equal"; which is one of its fundamental truths. It was not an accident that so many Masons signed the Declaration of Independence, or that Washington and most of his generals were members of the Order. Nor was it by mere chance that our first President was sworn into office on a Bible taken from a Masonic altar, by the Grand Master of New York.

Yet such facts—whereof we have a right to be proud—are but tokens of deeper facts, showing the place and power of Masonry in the making of our nation; as the fact that both Hamilton and Marshall were Masons reveals its part in forming our fundamental organic law. So much was this true that, in an evil hour, Masonry was made an issue in a political campaign, the result of which was the defeat of Henry Clay, because he was a Mason—and, incidentally, the election of Jackson, another Mason! Forever memorable is the fact that in the wild and fateful hour of Civil War, when states were torn in two and churches rent in twain—some of them not yet healed of the scars—the one tie that remained unbroken was the tie of Masonic fellowship. If Masonry could not prevent that saddest of all wars—setting church against church, family against family, and the nation against itself—it did mitigate its horror; and many a man in blue planted an acacia on the grave of a brother who wore the gray. Following the first day of battle at Gettysburg, there was a Lodge meeting in town, and Yanks and Rebs met and mingled under the Square and Compasses. If the story of Masonry in the war between the States is ever told, as surely it will be, it will melt our hearts with a new reverence for a Fraternity that built rainbow bridges of kindness from battle-line to battle-line, trying to heal the hurts of humanity. So it has been all down the years of our history, such facts being parables of much else; and today our Craft is worth more for the safety and sanctity of the Republic than either its army or its navy.

What of the present and the future? What will our country be like fifty years hence? Today we find ourselves in a new, strange, almost terrifying America, where wild forces are at play and alien influences are at work. For years we have been inundated by tides of immigration, not only from lands friendly to our institutions, but from others where our ideals are like an unknown tongue—multitudes lured by the glitter of gold, not by the beacon of liberty. They will be changed by America, but will not America, in turn, be changed by them into something different from what it has been and was meant to be? True, America should know nothing of the Saxon race, nothing of the Slavic race, but only the Human Race; but can we keep it true to its old and simple ideals in a medley of races, a confusion of events, in the eddies and cross-currents of this troubled time? These are questions which thoughtful Americans are everywhere asking, sometimes with alarm, often with dismay, as they watch the trend and tendency of affairs in which America is made the hunting-ground of every kind of propaganda—which only means that we must have a propaganda of our own, sanely, wisely, intelligently American, and here Masonry may find, and is finding, its great opportunity.

While Masonry abjures political questions and disputes in its Lodges, it is all the while training good citizens, and through the quality of its men —their character, their intelligence, their public-mindedness—it influences public and private life; as of old Washington, Franklin and Marshall wrought its spirit into our history. It is not politics that corrupts character; it is bad character that corrupts politics; and by building men up in spiritual faith and character, Masonry is helping to build the State that will endure the shocks of time—a nobler structure than was ever wrought of mortar or of marble. What we need more than all else is better character, born of a sense of duties as well as of rights; vigilant in behalf of liberty indeed as we must ever be, without sleeping and without holiday—but equally alert to see and seize the obligations which citizenship imposes. Only a little more than half of those entitled to vote ever vote on any issue—a fact which makes "government of the people, by the people, for the people" a farce! The ballot is our weapon of defense, our wand of power, and yet our people are so self-absorbed, so neglectful, that they forget or fail to use a power more sacred than the scepter of any king. If America is ever injured, it will be by Americans themselves—by their ignorance, their indifference, their neglect—and here again, Masonry can do fundamental work in quickening the sense of the duties of citizenship.

Ponder the problems now before the world—the limitation and final abolition of war; the snarling, snapping, racial rancor now so keenly felt in a world in which people are jammed together, and have not yet learned to live together;

the clash of class hatreds, which makes industry often look like a jungle; the demand for new feats of social engineering in behalf of education and the health of humanity; and, above all, the need of some unifying faith, or principle, to give coherence and cohesion to the world, that we may add a sagacious, forward-looking Human Providence to the mercy of a Divine Providence, making the future something different, something better, than the weary round of glory and a decay which tells the story of the past. Such are the problems now confronting the race, and the fourth dimension of every one of them is— Brotherhood, which is the very genius of Masonry; a Brotherhood based not on race, rank, or religion, but upon respect for the basic manhood which underlies the tawdry distinctions of caste and creed. Grim old Carlyle saw this long ago when he said:

"No revolution ever rises above the intellectual level of those who make it, and little is gained where one false notion supplants another. But we must, some day, at last and forever, cross the line between Nonsense and Commonsense. And on that day we shall pass from class paternalism, originally derived from fetish fiction in times of universal ignorance, to Human Brotherhood in accordance with the nature of things and our growing knowledge of it; from political government to industrial administration; from competition in individualism to individuality in cooperation; from war and despotism, in any form, to Peace and Liberty."

In America there is no excuse for poverty, no room for injustice, no reason for racial or sectarian rancor. It is the land of opportunity, of brotherhood, whose future is worth more than the time-stained story of any land, if it is true to its own ideals. Here, in this goodly gracious land, under a form of government which unites individual initiative with communal responsibility—liberty with law—men must be not only Builders but Brothers, sharing the large innocence of nature and the unfailing love of God, who cares more for a Brother than for a kingdom. Here, if we would have a philosophy, as well as an ethic, of fraternity, we must learn that goodness is fellowship, mutuality, service—in short, that it takes two men and God to make a brother. Here we must build and build together, joining hearts and hands with the Eternal Creative Good-will, each race adding its unique gift and vision to the common task and enterprise, if we would realize the greater America that is to be.

"The New Age stands as yet
Half built against the sky,

> Open to every threat
> Of storms that clamor by.
> Scaffolding veils the walls
> And dim dust floats and falls
> As moving to and fro, their tasks
> The Masons ply."

These things shall be—nay, they must be—else America will fail of her purpose and prophecy. In a land where there is plenty for all, room for all—room for everything except hatred—God has ordained that we build a Beloved Community in which there is freedom and justice for all, because each is loyal and faithful in the service of the common good. Not otherwise may we know the worth and meaning of our individual lives—so brief at their longest, so broken at their best—save as we see them and use them in the fellowship of the large purpose of the wise Master Builder. Brotherhood is inevitable. Its foundations are laid in the order of the world. Its pillars stand up proudly on either side. It is the will and purpose of God, as it is the duty and destiny of man. It is the genius of America and the soul of Masonry.

> "The wind of God is blowing
> Through the open minds of men,
> And His sharp share is plowing
> In the troubled hearts of men;

And soon there'll be a sowing,
And a springing and a growing,
And then a new grace flowing
Through all the lives of men.
For so shall come God's harvest home
In the ripening souls of men."

Chapter XIII

THE CORNERSTONE OF THE FUTURE [1]

All of us deeply regret the absence of the President, and equally the private anxiety which has detained him. For, much as we honor his counselors, nobody can take the place of the President. When he is a candidate for office he is one of ourselves, and we inspect him rather carefully. When he is elected, he is something more, and we need not apologize to any sentiment of equality for regarding him with reverence. He wears upon his shoulders the vestiture of the will and purpose of a great people. What he does we do through him. He is our spokesman and leader, as well as our friend. From the bottom of our hearts we say, God save the President!

Every Masonic occasion is a patriotic occasion. It has ever been the genius of our ancient and gentle Craft to respect constituted authority, and

[1] The laying of the Cornerstone of the new Masonic Temple in Detroit, Sept. 18th, 1922, must be accounted a great day in American Masonry. President Harding had promised to be present, but was detained by the illness of Mrs. Harding. Hon. Edwin Denby, Secretary of the Navy, presided as Toastmaster, which explains the opening paragraph of the address.

133

to be the friend of all noble government, wherever its labors call it. The first President of our Republic was a Mason, as is the man who sits in his chair in the White House to-day. All through the thrilling story of America it has been the purpose and labor of Freemasonry to exalt, purify and transfigure the national spirit, and to apply a moral patriotism to private life and public service.

Surely this is a memorable day. With imposing parade and impressive ceremonies the cornerstone of the new Temple has been laid in due and ancient form. It is a notable day not only in the Masonic history of Detroit, but in the Masonic annals of the nation. Blessed by the President, the cement spread by the trowel of Washington, in the presence of the greatest assembly of Masons in modern times, in one of the most brilliant cities in the world—truly, it is a Cornerstone of the Future. Standing so near the invisible and unguarded border between the United States and the Dominion of Canada, the new uprising Cathedral of Brotherhood will be a tie and a meeting-place between English-speaking peoples, into whose history a common and great Freemasonry is so deeply woven, and upon whose civilization and destiny it has had so benign an influence.

For some of us this day, so perfect in its

THE CORNERSTONE OF THE FUTURE 135

arrangements and so solemnly joyous in its spirit, has a double meaning. As a cornerstone unites two walls, making for union and strength, so the new Temple joins the past and the future. It is a dream of the past come true, the crown and climax of the faithful, aspiring and consecrated labors of years agone. Our fathers builded better than they knew, laying the foundations on which the Temple rests; and we must build the future with equal care, uniting practical wisdom with prophetic vision. After all, the Temple is but the outward and visible sign of an inward grace and power, and our problem now is to make our Masonry as great as its Temple. A little Masonry may dwell in a great Temple, and a great Masonry may live in a little Upper Room over a shop or a store. In the things that matter most size does not signify, and numbers do not count; the spirit is the one thing needful. Without it all else is an elaborate insignificance, an imposing vacuity. What makes Masonry great is its profound faith, its moral idealism, its sincere fellowship, its fruitful and practical service to the common good.

The story of Masonry is one of the great romances of the world. Older than our Republic, older than any living religion, it has come to us out of the mists of the past, one of the holiest institutions known to mankind. Next to the home, the state, and the house of God, it has been a creative and blessed influence in the making of mankind. On the occasion of the laying of the cornerstone of what is to be one of the noblest Masonic temples on earth, under whose high and hospitable roof every form of Freemasonry will find shelter and work together, we may well think, if only for a brief time, of what Freemasonry is, renewing both our vision and our vows.

As all things Masonic are divided into three parts, so Masonry itself may be divided. There is, first of all, universal craft Masonry, having its basis and background in the history of the ancient Builders, who were also poets, whose cathedrals—poems wrought in stone—consecrate the world. Cryptic Masonry is a part of Craft Masonry, and is only a further elaboration and exposition of the symbolism of the building of the Temple—using the tools of the builder as symbols of the thoughts of the thinker. All Craft Masonry has to do with the building of the individual man. It works at the foundations. It may be a truism that the world can never be better than the men in it; nevertheless it is true. Our dreams end in delusion because there are not men enough who are good enough to make them come true. Masonry seeks to lay the foundation of social life in noble private character, in that simple and fundamental morality which is the stairway by which men ascend into the House of the Lord.

Nothing in Masonry is more beautiful than its first degree. It teaches us the basic principles of righteousness upon which all else depends, as the second degree urges that intellectual culture without which manhood is rudimentary. Since we are under a moral obligation to be intelligent, we must study the "arts and sciences," the better to know the order of the world in which we live and the laws of the Master Builder. The third degree is one of the most profound and thrilling dramas on earth, seeking to initiate us, symbolically, into the Eternal Life. Morality, intelligence, and a sense of the Life Everlasting—these three things Craft Masonry seeks to teach us, training us in the eternal verities which are the basis of a noble, refined and valiant manhood.

As Craft Masonry deals with the making of individual character, so the Scottish Rite has to do with the development of society—the organization of personal righteousness into social ministry and world order. It is philosophy taught in picture. It dramatizes the ultimate truth, so far as man can know it, bringing parable, symbol and emblem to the service of that ineffable vision, veiled in silence and fringed with splendor, which gives worth and meaning to mortal life. For richness of suggestion, for beauty of poetic imagery, it is difficult to imagine anything more resplendent than the degrees of the Ancient and Accepted Rite. It is a great temple where truth is divested of superstition, and men learn in fellowship what none may know alone.

By the same token, it was in accord with the fitness of things that two such beautiful things as Christianity and Freemasonry should be brought together; and that was done in the stately order of the Knights Templar. It rescued from oblivion the gallant chivalry of the Middle Ages, in which courage was dedicated to the service of the truth and the defense of the weak, adding an indefinable grace, which is the unique gift of Christianity, to the fellowship of Masonry.

Again, Mr. Toastmaster, let me divide my subject into three parts. As there are three forms of Freemasonry, so there are three services which Masonry should render to America. Some of us believe in America, as we believe in God, and we believe that the future of the world, in a degree not yet realized, will depend upon a true-hearted, clear-seeing America. God made America unique, bringing all races and creeds together under one flag to learn fraternity and fellowship. America must not repeat on a

THE CORNERSTONE OF THE FUTURE

gigantic scale the blunders of the past; it must do something that has never been done before. Here, by the mercy of God, we must create and cultivate a spirit free, friendly and fraternal, to sweeten the bitterness of the world and heal its ancient hates.

The first great service which Masonry, by its genius no less than its history, can render to America, is to help heal it of racial rancor. Wells was right when he said that racial rancor is the most terrible thing on earth. It has in it the seeds of friction and endless feud. It is present to an alarming degree in all our great cities, like New York and Detroit, and it bodes no good for our country. It poisons private fellowship and pollutes public life. All through our national life it is an undertone of irritation, making for ill-will and confusion—a danger that may easily be a disaster. It is the first principle of Masonry that it estimates a man not by his race, but by his character and worth as a man. To-day, as never before, Masonry must hold its fundamental truth aloft as a light to guide, a spirit to inspire, and a wisdom to lead. A blind, unreasoning racial rancor must give way to the light of intelligence, if we are not to live in a welter of wrangling hatreds and hideous conflicts—a future which no one can contemplate without dismay.

Next to racial rancor, religious bigotry is the most horrible scourge of history, and, alas, we are not free from it. Everywhere, on all sides, it befogs insight and distorts judgment, turning fellowship into feud and faith into fanaticism. Masonry, by all the obligations of its history and genius, must build a wall against this evil, the story of which is stained with blood and blotted with tears. We must not allow any set of men to "Ulsterize" America, and repeat in our cities such scenes as have terrified the streets of Belfast. Least of all must Masonry be used as a weapon with which to fight any religion. Indeed, it may be taken as an axiom that men who fight about religion have no religion to fight about. The saying of Penn, so beloved by Lincoln, is a perfect statement of the historic attitude of Masonry: "All just men, all devout men, are everywhere of one religion, and when death hath taken off the masks they will know one another." But why wait for death to remove the masks? Masonry teaches no religion save that religion of all good men which underlies all sects and out-tops all creeds.

By that fact, Mr. Toastmaster, the supreme service of Masonry to America lies in the cultivation of the spiritual quality in our national life. It is for us to build a bulwark not only against hatred and bigotry, but also, and much more, against materialism. Here is our great temptation as a nation. Just now our friends in Europe feel resentment against us because we are rich. America is rich. God made it rich. The fabulous resources of the country make it rich. We did not get rich out of the war, as our friends abroad imagine. Nobody got rich out of the war. New York cannot be made rich by burning Chicago down. No, America has always been rich, and that is both its power and its peril. Because of the ever-present lure of materialism, we must be the more alert and sagacious in keeping a clean flame of spiritual vision aglow in our hearts, that we may rightly discriminate among the values of life. Without moral idealism, without spiritual leadership, America will lose its way. America must build a Beloved Community in this New World, and Freemasonry, by its moral insight and spiritual fellowship, must be one of the builders.

To such high tasks our Fraternity is dedicated; upon such foundations the cornerstone of the Temple is laid. When, at last, by the mercy of God and the skill of the Builders, the Temple is finished, adorned, and consecrated, and we see it standing stately in the sunlight, or touched by the soft mysticism of the night, the humblest craftsman will be as proud and happy as the highest officer; and men will come from all over the land, and from beyond the seas, to wonder and admire, thanking God for a great central shrine of fraternal righteousness, spiritual faith, and patriotic loyalty—an Altar of Good-will uplifted in a day when the brotherhood of the world is broken.

Chapter XIV

THE FLAG OF PEACE

'Tis said that the Flag of our Republic was born in 1777, but that cannot be true. It was stitched into form at that time in a little back parlor, but he who would know its origin must look far into the dim, pathetic, aspiring past. It was woven on the Loom of Ages—woven of the dreams and heartbeats of humanity, of the warp of sorrow and the woof of hope—by a Great Hand stretched out from the Unseen. All those who on red fields of war died that their sons might be free; all who in dark prison cells suffered for the rights of man; all who in the long night of tyranny toiled and prayed for a better day, added threads to our Flag. It floats to-day in the blue sky, swayed by happy winds, held aloft by innumerable hands of the living and the dead, at once a history and a prophecy.

In old mythology Minerva and Ceres presided over the laboring classes—robed in flaming red, and that color became their emblem; but it was an emblem of blood-making, not of blood-letting, symbolizing the victories of peace, not those of war. Color in ancient Rome separated plebeian from patrician—blue the color of the aristocracy, white the war symbol, and red the emblem of labor and peace. All these colors are blended in our Flag, making it the sanctifying symbol of Unity, Fraternity, and Good-will among men. So may it ever be—Flag of Freedom and Friendship—woven of "the mystic chords of memory, stretching from every battlefield and patriot grave to every living heart and hearthstone all over this broad land," proclaiming the time-glorified principles wrought out by the tears and prayers of our fathers.

Let all those who stand under it join hearts in one faith, join hands in one purpose—for the safety and sanctity of this Republic; for the rights of man and the majesty of law; for the moral trusteeship of private property and public office; for the education of the ignorant; for the lifting of poverty, through self-help, to comfort; for the dignity of the home and the laughter of little children; for social beauty, national glory, and human welfare. Long may it wave, rendered for all ages holy by the faith of the men who lifted it up, and the valor of the men who defended it in an hour of madness and peril. May it never again float over a field of war, but ever and forever over scenes of peace, honor, and progress.

PART THREE: *Personalities*

Chapter XV

THE SPIRIT OF ROBERT BURNS[1]

We are met this evening, as I understand it, just to love Robert Burns and one another. Somehow I feel that Burns would rejoice to be here, for he loved more than all else that festival that was half a frolic and the feast where joy and good-will were guests. The social magnetism of his spirit found its way into his songs, and we feel it to this day, and he was nowhere more happy, nowhere more welcome, than in the fellowship of his Masonic Brethren. Higher tribute there is none for any man than to say, justly, that the world is gentler and more joyous for his having lived—and that was true of Burns, whose very name is an emblem of pity, joy, and the genius of fraternity. And it is therefor that we love Robert Burns, as much for his weakness as for his strength, and all the more for that he was such an unveneered human being. If he

[1] Address delivered in proposing the toast "To the Immortal Memory of Bro. Robert Burns," at the Burns Meeting of the Scots Lodge, No. 2319, English Constitution, London, 24th January, 1918.

was a sinner, he was in that akin to ourselves, as God wots, a little good and a little bad, a little weak and a little strong, foolish when he thought he was wise, and wise, often, when he feared he was foolish. It is given but to few men thus to live in the hearts of their fellows; and, to-day, from Ayr to Sidney, from Chicago to Calcutta, the memory of Burns is a sweet perfume. Yes, more than a fragrance, it is a living force uniting men of many lands, by a kind of Freemasonry, into a league of liberty, justice, and pity.

There is a certain fitness in a man of my country proposing this toast to the Memory of Robert Burns. Mark Twain, the Lincoln of our literature, used to say that our American Civil War was a fight between Sir Walter Scott and Robert Burns. Of course, it was an exaggeration, but none the less a picturesque way of stating a fact. We of the South read Sir Walter Scott for his pride of blood and extraction, for his grace and charm of courtesy, for his pictures of an old romantic feudalism—and, I may add, for the strength and sweetness of his genius. Our Southern society, for all its culture and hospitality, was the old feudalism transplanted to the New World. The Yankees read Robert Burns, who said that "a man's a man for a' that," whether white or black or brown. That

THE SPIRIT OF ROBERT BURNS

is to say, our Civil War was a clash of ideals, each growing and struggling to be free, an old feudalism against a new uprising democracy of which Burns was the God-endowed prophet. And so the conflict was inevitable.

About the walls of Troy, as Homer saw it, two battles raged, one on the earth between Greeks and Trojans, one in the viewless air between gods and goddesses. So to-day, above the long, winding, ragged lines of the greatest of all wars, two battles are raging—a battle of guns and a battle of ideals. It is a conflict of two conceptions of life and civilization which cannot live together on this earth and keep the peace; and we are struggling together to decide which ideal shall shape the destination of mankind. One in arts and aims and ideals, and now, at last, one in arms, the land of Lincoln and the land of Burns are fighting for the fundamental truths which Burns set to everlasting music.

Some there are who dream of a vague blur of cosmopolitanism, in which all local loyalties, all heroic national genius shall be merged and forgotten. Not so Burns. He was distinctively a national poet, striking deep roots into his native soil, and, for that very reason, touching a chord so haunting that it echoes forever. When Burns appeared the spirit of Scotland was at a low ebb. Her people were crushed and her ancient fire almost quenched. Her scholars blushed to be convicted of a Scottism in speech. It was at such a time that Burns came, inspired by the history of his people, the traditions of Wallace and Bruce stirring him like a passion, his soul attuned to the ancient ballads of love and daring, singing the simple life of his nation in their vivid and simple language. He struck with a delicate but strong hand the deep and noble feelings of his countrymen, and somewhere upon his variegated robe of song will be found embroidered the life, the faith, the genius of his people. He made it a double honor to be a Scotsman. It is therefor that the men of Scotland love him, as, perhaps, never people loved a poet, and make his home at once a throne of melody and a shrine of national glory.

"The Memory of Burns," cried Emerson, "I am afraid heaven and earth have taken too good care of it to leave us anything to say. The west winds are murmuring it. Open the windows behind you and hearken to the incoming tide, what the waves say of it. The doves perching on the eaves of a stone chapel opposite may know something about it. The Memory of Burns—every man's, every boy's, every girl's head carries snatches of his songs, and they say them by heart; and, what is strangest of all, never learned them from a book, but from mouth to mouth.

They are the property and the solace of mankind."

If ever of any one, it can be said of Robert Burns, that his soul goes marching on, striding over continents and years, trampling tyrannies down. He was the harbinger of the nineteenth century, the poet of the rights and reign of the common people, whom, it has been said, God must love because He made so many of them. The earth was fresh upon the tomb of Washington when that century was born; it discovered Lincoln and buried him with infinite regret. Indeed, had Burns reached his four-score years, he might have known our peasant-President; he surely must have known him by fame and warm appreciation. In this way Lincoln knew him and fondly repeated the somber stanzas of "Man Was Made to Mourn," because it suited the temper of his melancholy spirit. But the victorious melody of the age of Lincoln first found voice in the songs of Burns, as the Greek singer inspired Petrarch with the fire that forced the Renascence, and out of the inertia of the Middle Ages created modern times. So, when Taine came to account for that age he found that its spirit "broke first in a Scotch peasant, Robert Burns" —a man of all men most fitted to give it voice, because "scarcely ever was seen together more of misery and of talent."

This is not the time to rattle the dry bones of literary criticism—a dreary business at best, and a dismal business at worst. It is by all agreed that Robert Burns was a lyric poet of the first order, if not the greatest song-writer of the world. Draw a line from Shakespeare to Browning, and he is one of the few tall enough to touch it. The qualities of Burns are simplicity, naturalness, vividness, fire, sweet-toned pathos, and rollicking humor—qualities rare enough and still more rarely blended. But he was a man first, and his fame rests upon verses written swiftly, as men write letters, and upon songs that were as spontaneous, as artless, and as lovely as the songs of birds. But the spirit of Burns was not merely local. His passion for liberty, his affirmation of the nobility of man, his sense of the dignity of labor, his pictures of the beauties of nature, of the pathos and hard lot of the lowly, of the joys and woes and pieties of his people find response in every breast where beats the heart of a man. Surely no one, since the Son of Man lodged with the fishermen by the sea, has taught more clearly the brotherhood of man and the kinship of all breathing things.

That which lives in Robert Burns, and will live while human nature is the same, is his love of justice, of honesty, his touch of pathos, of melting sympathy, his demand for liberty, his faith in man, in nature, and in God—all uttered with simple speech and the golden voice of song. His poems were little jets of love and liberty and pity finding their way out through the fissures in the granite-like theology of his day. They came fresh from the heart of a man whom the death of a little bird set dreaming of the meaning of a world wherein life is woven of beauty, mystery, and sorrow. A flower crushed in the budding, a field mouse turned out of its home by a plowshare, a wounded hare limping along the road to dusty death, or the memory of a tiny bird who sang for him in days agone, touched him to tears. His poems did not grow: they awoke complete. He was a child of the open air, and about all his songs there is an outdoor feeling. He saw Nature with the swift glances of a child—saw beauty in the fold of clouds, in the slant of trees, in the lilt and glint of flowing waters, in the immortal game of hide-and-seek played by sunbeams and shadows, in the mists trailing over the hills. The sigh of the wind in the forest filled him with a kind of wild, sad joy, and the tender face of a mountain daisy was like the thought of one much loved and long dead. So the throb of his heart is warm in his words, and it was a heart in which he carried an alabaster box of pity. He had a sad life and a soul of fire, the instincts of an angel in the midst of hard poverty; yet he lived with dash and daring, sometimes with folly, and, we must add—else we do not know Burns—with a certain bubbling joyousness, a lyric glee as of a bird singing in the boughs.

Such was the spirit of Robert Burns—a man passionate and piteous, compact of light and flame and beauty, capable of withering scorn of wrong, quickly shifting from the ludicrous to the horrible, poised between laughter and tears—and if by some art we could send it into all the dark places of the world, pity and joy would return to the common ways of man. Long live the Spirit of Robert Burns. May it grow and glow to the confounding of all unkindness, all injustice, all bitterness.

> "He haunts his native land
>   As an immortal youth; his hand
>   Guides every plough.
>   His presence haunts this room to-night
>   A form of mingled mist and light
>   From that far-coast."

His feet may be in the furrow, but the nobility of manhood is in his heart, on his lips the voice of eternal melody, and in his face the light of the morning star. I give you the toast, "To the Immortal Memory of Robert Burns!"

Chapter XVI
"FATHER" TAYLOR

Robert Collyer tells of attending a prayer meeting one bright May morning in the old Hollis Street church, Boston. Cyrus Bartol—author of that remarkable book called *Radical Problems*—was the leader, and after a brief pause in the meeting he spoke to a man well on in years who was sitting on a front seat who rose to his feet. There was a rustle in the meeting, and a light of expectation in all faces, like the breath which touches the leaves in a garden. Collyer bent forward and heard a strangely sweet voice speaking about Doves. He had seen them that morning on his way to the meeting, crowding to a window to be fed by some friendly hand, and the sight reminded him of the words of the prophet: "Who are these that fly as doves to the window?"

As the speaker warmed to his theme, the old church seemed to be full of doves—one could hear the soft whirr of their wings. They came crowding in from the New England woods and the dove cotes at the North End—doves of the prophet's time, white and purple, out of the heavens and into the heavens. Then somehow those who listened were doves, come at the Father's call that morning to be fed from his hand, or longing to plume their wings and fly away and be at rest. It was the enchantment of pure genius—a pentecost of flying doves—and Collyer wist not who had wrought the wonder. So he asked a man who sat near him who it was, and the man answered, astonished that any one in Boston should ask such a question, "Why, that is Father Taylor!"

Collyer was a young man, and after the meeting Bartol introduced him to Father Taylor. The lad held out his hand shyly, and the old man did not offer his in return. Instead, he opened his great arms, caught the boy in a warm embrace, and kissed him. Thereafter they were friends to the end. That was Father Taylor—"Jeremy Taylor in butternut," as Harriet Martineau called him—and the only man on this side of the sea Charles Dickens went to hear on his first visit; the man who charmed Jenny Lind, the elder Booth, Webster, Emerson, Everett, and all who heard him; and whose smile was so bright that his little daughter made up her mind that this was what made the flowers open in their living room.

Edward Taylor was born on Christmas day

in Richmond, Virginia, 1793—into a forlorn world, because his mother, a Scotch governess, passed out of life as he came in. The little "bundle of a baby" fell into the care of a black mammy, whose love and gentleness ever after haunted his heart. Like Moses, drawn out of the bulrush ark, he was a foundling of providence, dowered with the mysterious power we call genius. He was a ruddy child, as of red earth the first Adam was made—a sort of lion, if one looked at him through the glasses of Darwin, but a lamb also, having the subtlety of the serpent in his intellect and the sweet foolishness of the dove in his heart. Like the elder Booth who wanted prayers over some dead pigeons, so Taylor held funeral services over chickens and kittens who departed this life, and used not only persuasion, but a whip, to gather his audience of pickaninnies and put them in proper frame of mind—though the lash was doubtless as gentle as the oratory was wonderful. When he was seven he was one day picking up chips for the good woman to whom the charge of him had fallen, when a sea-captain passing by asked him if he did not want to be a sailor. Instantly he left the chips, ran to the house and shouted, "Good-by, mother," and was off to sea as cabin boy.

In the biography of Taylor—by Gilbert Haven

and Thomas Russell—the next ten years are called "a blank," and they were no doubt a hard experience, to which he rarely referred. Years later when he was taken by a friend to visit Dr. W. E. Channing, on leaving the house he observed to the friend, "Channing has splendid talents; what a pity he has not been educated!" By which he meant, no doubt, that there is a kind of education not to be obtained from books —such as he had acquired in the university of winds and waves, through whose long and trying curriculum, with many sharp examinations, he had passed. For ten years he endured hardness as a good sailor, and we next see him wandering on a Sunday morning into the Park Street church, Boston, and leaving it with a hunger in his heart to be able some day to appeal to men like the great preacher he heard there.

Another Sabbath found him in a Methodist chapel, and his heart was strangely moved by one who probed to the depths of that latent conscience and remorse which probably lie somewhere in the background of every soul. As he was going out a good man grasped his hand— as Methodists have a way of doing—and asked him about his soul. This was a double surprise, for the boy wanted human sympathy and here it was, and he was not aware until then that he had such a thing as a soul. And the upshot of it was that he was converted in the good old Methodist way—that is, converted all over, set on fire, all icicles melted and all sins burned up. It was the memory of this high and sunny hour that led him to tell his Unitarian friends that they were trying to raise wheat in the Arctic Circle, and that they might as well try to heat a furnace with snowballs as to save souls in their way.

In the war of 1812 Taylor went to sea on the *Black Hawk,* a privateer. She was soon captured by our friends the enemy, and her crew were sent as prisoners to Halifax, Nova Scotia. There was a rebellion among the boys when the chaplain read the prayers to them for King George, so they would not hear him. Taylor was known to be "a praying man" and he was asked to take the chaplain's place. He was quick and ready to do this, and after a time it dawned upon the boys that one who could pray so well might also preach, because, as they argued, it was only the difference between talking on your knees and on your feet. But Taylor could not read and he was puzzled about finding a text. The problem was easily solved. They found a Bible and one of the boys would read at haphazard until some text struck fire. So, reading one day, they came upon the words, "A good child is better than a foolish old king," and Taylor said, "That will do for a text," and he launched out into a story of our glorious Revolution, set them all afire, and came down heavily on foolish old King George to the vast delight of his audience. From that time he was chaplain on a prisoner's ration while the other man drew the pay.

Released from prison, the young apostle could not hide his light under a bushel—for that would have burnt the bushel, so he became an exhorter at the meetings on Methodist Alley. And the good Methodists—wise in this as in many things—were for giving him a license as a local preacher, despite the fact that he could not read; and two church officers were sent to hear him. Taylor was not supposed to know of their presence, but a kind friend told him, and he took for his text, "By the life of Pharaoh ye are spies." All the same he was licensed to preach on a salary of nothing a year and board himself—the conditions on which I preached the first year of my ministry, and I am sure now that I got the best of the bargain! To make his board Taylor hired out to a peddler in Ann Street, who sent him down the coast with a load of tin notions. He came to Saugus in his journey, disposed of his wares, and then was moved to preach—sold his tins first, mark you, and preached afterward, not before—and won the heart of a dear old lady, who took him to her home, taught him how to read, and gave him the love of a mother. Later Amos Binney tried to send him to a theological school, but he stayed only six weeks and could stand it no longer.

So a full license was given him, and he was sent to Marblehead to take charge of an infant church there. And there he met Deborah, a maid to win the love of any man, and soon the young prophet was vastly in love. Shortly after he was moved to Hingham—four miles away—and one day he went up on the hill to gaze toward Marblehead, with a telescope to assist his heart, when in a flash the thought struck him and he leaped to his feet with the cry, "Bless my heart, this is our wedding day and I forgot all about it!" It was long after the hour set, but Deborah knew that if Edward ran he would run only one way. Still, one wishes that we had a report of their meeting next morning, to see how genius rose to the high demand when he told her how it was. They were married, and there was no need for the minister to say "for better or worse," for there was no worse—it was all and always for the better.

At Duxbury, where he and Deborah lived, he disturbed the long-enduring slumber of that fine old town, and some of the ministers were jealous of him. One of the ministers—the Unitarian pastor, meeting Taylor on the street, said, "So, young man, ye have come to preach in Duxbury, have ye?" "Yes," replied the young man, "the Lord bid us preach the gospel to every creature." "To be sure," snorted the old man, "but he never said every critter should preach the gospel, sir," and went away in wrath. And next Sunday Taylor prayed that every white hair on that old man's head might be hung with a jewel of the Lord. He also prayed, specifically, that the Lord might "bless meek Burr, and proud Pratt, and save wicked old Alden, if you can!"

About this time, 1828, the good Methodists began to feel concern for those "who go down to the sea in ships," and it was surely the good God who guided them in selecting Edward Taylor for this ministry. He began in a dingy chapel on Methodist Alley, but the room was soon too small—many people from fashionable churches going to hear a man with a golden voice and a heart of fire. Nathaniel Barret, a Unitarian layman, wrote notes to a hundred of his friends, mainly of that faith, calling them together. He laid the matter before them, and it was decided to build a new meeting house for Taylor. So the Unitarians built a chapel for the Methodist evangelist, and that was in accord with the eternal fitness of things. They asked Taylor what he wanted, and he said they might leave out the Corinthian columns and give him the shavings.

But they gave him, instead, of their best, and that was none too good.

The chapel was built in the shape of a ship, in dark finish, with low ceiling, ample and inviting. Behind the pulpit an artist hung a painting of a ship in distress, storm-tossed and driven. Taylor called this temple "Bethel," remembering the ladder of Jacob whereon angels ascended and descended in a dream that was also a prayer. And Edward Everett called Taylor himself "a walking Bethel." Two sailor boys stood in front of the chapel one day, and one who could spell proceeded to make out the name over the door: "B-e-t, that's beat; H-e-l, that's hell, here's where the old man beats hell, let's go in." And they came in numbers, a wilderness of wild human souls, and the genius of Taylor shone like a beacon in the night. But so many others came that he had to make a rule that the sailor boys should be seated first, and if they filled the seats the rest must stand. Sailor Jack saw the point, and sat on his dignity.

To the sailor boys he was a friend and father, and so it came about that he was called "Father" Taylor—and a higher tribute was never paid to a Christian minister. Taylor had the freedom of the city. He knocked at every door, Orthodox, Episcopal, Catholic or Radical, and everywhere he was welcome, and everywhere he was at home, being large enough and wise enough to see the good in every faith. By the same token, he would have no doors to his pulpit, and one day when a minister refused to enter because Henry Ware, a Unitarian, was to sit there—a way some men had in those days of proving that they were Christians, by failing to be gentlemen —Taylor prayed fervently: "Lord, there are two things we need to be delivered from in Boston —bad rum and bigotry. Which is the worst Thou knowest, I don't, Amen." When some one said in his hearing that Emerson would surely go to hell, he cried out: "Go there! Why, if he went there he would change the climate and the tide of emigration would set in that way."

Taylor was early interested in Freemasonry, having joined the Corner Stone Lodge at Duxbury, as the records reveal, March 6th, 1820; and he loved and served the Order to the day of his death. In the days of the anti-Masonic fanaticism, when many withdrew in terror from the Fraternity, and its members often slunk into its meetings hastily, with caps pulled down over their faces, Taylor used to strut into the entrance with his hat tilted back on what he called his "organ of obstinacy." Good Bishop Hedding —under whose obedience, as a Methodist, he labored—tried to stop Taylor from marching in Masonic processions, to avoid occasion for stumbling, but to no avail. He marched all the more boldly, and the Bishop said in despair: "Well, Eddy will wear his apron in spite of us." Taylor was afterwards a member of Columbian Lodge, Boston, constant in his attendance, and his prayer at the opening of the Lodge when the anti-Masonic excitement was at its height, was never forgotten: "O Lord, bless this glorious Order; bless its friends; yea, bless its enemies, and make their hearts as soft as their heads. Amen." He was also a Knight Templar of the Boston Commandery, and one of the most beloved of the Grand Chaplains of the Grand Lodge of Massachusetts.

Of all American orators he was the most original and inimitable in his genius and style. If you would know by what spell he swayed men, the cultured equally with the unlearned, read the little essay on *Father Taylor* by Walt Whitman, in *November Boughs*. There you will see, as far as such things can be put into words, why it was that great actors when they came to see "how he did it," forgot what they came for and retreated behind their pocket-handkerchiefs to hide their sobs. There were great orators in Boston—Everett with his studious grace, Webster with his majesty, and Choate with his oriental fancy—but no one carried men away in a chariot of fire as Taylor did; and this power in him surprised no one more than it did himself. He was a possessed man, and in his rapt moods he became a live transparency in which men saw those things of which it is not lawful to speak. And, joined with this, was that winged wit, that fine and sure sanity, that common sense which his heavenly genius glorified. Here are some of his sayings:

"A man should not preach like he had killed somebody," he said when a brother was too solemn.

He compared getting ready to preach to fermentation: "When the liquor begins to swell and strain and hum and fizz, then pull the bung!"

"When a man is preaching at me I want him to take something hot out of his own heart and shove it into mine—that is what I call preaching."

One day, preaching on amusements, he paid eulogy to Jenny Lind as "the sweetest song-bird that ever alighted on our shores." A man sitting on the pulpit steps asked if a person dying at one of her concerts would go to heaven. Taylor's eyes became two points of green fire, and he said: "A good man will go to heaven, sir, die where he may, and a fool will be a fool wherever he lives, though he sits on my pulpit stairs."

A man caught in the Millerite craze insisted on

telling the sailor boys to get their ascension robes ready, as the world was coming to an end, and Taylor cried out, "Cut his boot-straps and let him go up, so the meeting can go on!"

"Emerson, I think, is the sweetest soul God ever made, but he knows no more about theology than Balaam's ass knew about Hebrew grammar. There seems to be a screw loose in him somewhere, but I never could find it, and listen as I may, I can find no jar in the machinery."

To a minister who had taught the dogma of infant damnation, he said: "It's no use, brother, preaching sermons like that, because if what you say could be true, your God would be my devil."

"Webster is too bad to trust with anything good now, and too good to throw away; he is the best bad man I ever knew."

"Niagara is like the love of God; it never freezes up in winter, never dries up in dog days, and you never come to it for water and go away with an empty bucket."

And so, like a Niagara, the stream of his wit and wisdom flowed on, leaping, sparkling, and seemingly inexhaustible, until it emptied into the great sea. In April, 1871, he passed on—or over, as the French say—going out with the ebbing tide, as "an old salt" should. Just before he died some one said: "There is rest in heaven, and you will soon be there."

"Go there yourself," he said, "I want to stay here."

"But think of the angels, all waiting to welcome you," he was told.

"I don't want angels, I want folks." And then in an instant the old radiance returned and he said: "Angels are folks, too, and ours are among them."

So passed the waif, sailor, privateersman, prisoner, and preacher—a big, fiery, fatherly, joyous man whose heart God had touched—and Boston paid honor to one of her first citizens, if not to the greatest natural orator that ever lived. And there was sorrow on the sea, for many a sailor boy felt a lump climb into his throat and a strange tightening about the heart when he learned that Father Taylor was no more.

Chapter XVII

EDWIN MARKHAM

Among the poets of America now living there is none greater, alike in personal character and wealth of genius, than Edwin Markham, who is the noblest Masonic singer since Robert Burns. Sweet of heart, with a mind full of benign light, he sings of the old simplicities and sanctities which must lie at the basis of individual worth and social welfare, the while he teaches us to see and to follow "that thread of all-sustaining Beauty that runs through all and doth all unite." He is, indeed, the supreme poet, since Whitman, of the goodly, gracious gospel of Brotherly Love so much needed in the world now and always. Here follows a brief sketch of the man, with an appreciation of his genius as a singer and a seer.

There is nothing for surprise that such a man descends from a sturdy ancestry, both intellectual and moral. On his paternal side his lineage runs back to Colonel Markham, the first cousin and secretary of William Penn, and later acting-governor of Pennsylvania. His maternal line, through the Winchells, runs back into the best stock of New and Old England and Holland. Our poet was born in Oregon, in 1852, whither his pioneer parents had moved from Michigan. His father dying when the boy was little more than four years of age, we find him living with his mother and brother in one of the remote romantic valleys of California. His mother was a woman of rather silent nature—his brother was deaf and dumb—and the lad was left much alone with nature and his own inner life. Years of quiet brooding, while he followed the cattle or folded the sheep, developed depth and originality of mind, evoking the poet-soul within him. Memories of those days when he was a shepherd boy find echo in his poems, as, for example, in "The Heart's Return."

Partly, at least, his gift of song was an inheritance, for his mother, albeit so quiet and reserved, was a lover of poetry and a writer of verse on her own account. Some of her lines were frequently to be found in the papers of the time. The first money that Edwin earned was twenty-five dollars for plowing a neighbor's field, which his mother told him was his, and that he might have whatever he wished to buy with it. He bought books—Webster's Unabridged Dictionary, and the poems of Tennyson, Bryant and Moore. It is not difficult to imagine the use to which he put those precious volumes in the leisure that was his in the peaceful valley of Suisun, where he tended the flocks and herds. His chance for early technical training was slight —about three months in the year, and not always that—but he studied diligently, making the best use of whatever books came his way. Also, he worked and dreamed and laid plans, in such various ways as ambitious boys can devise, until at eighteen he entered the State Normal School at San José, and later finished his school work at Christian College, Santa Rosa. Believing in the value of handicraft, he mastered the secrets of blacksmithing and wrought at the forge for a time. But a man of his genius was not allowed to remain at the forge, and he was soon called to other and higher service.

Markham was made a Mason in Acacia Lodge No. 92, at Coloma, California, in the early eighties, and he has an abiding interest in the Order. From the first the Spirit of Masonry moved him deeply, as was natural for a man to whom Brotherhood is not only "the crest and crowning of all good," but religion in its deeper name, and who sees that

> "The fine audacities of honest deed,
> The homely old integrities of soul,"

must be the foundation alike of personal character and social beauty. He reckons Masonry among the deep, quiet, beautiful forces destined to soften the hard winter of the world into a great summer time of friendship and good-will. Of one who is so chaste of soul, so aglow with the joy of life and the wonder of the world, and so brotherly withal, it may be said that he has found the Master's Word. His friend Joaquin Miller said of him years ago:

> "Markham has always seemed to me the purest of the pure; the cleanest-minded man of all the many great and good of his high calling I have known, and it has been my high privilege to know nearly all of the great authors of Saxon lands this last third of a century."

With Markham poetry is not a byplay, nor a soft sensuous sentimentality, but a high and heavenly vocation, the fit vehicle for the expression of the truths that make us men. There is something of the urge of divine necessity in all his song, and a sense of consecration. It is the prophetic element that one feels in his music, as of a man who has heard unutterable things and must speak. One cannot read "The Whirlwind Road," for instance, without being reminded of St. Paul and the company of those who lived the dedicated life. For him the home of the poet is on the heights, and his mission is one of leadership—no "idle singer of an empty day," but a pilot voice foretelling a new day:

> "Life is a mission stern as fate,
> And song a dread apostolate.
> The toils of prophecy are his,
> To hail the coming centuries—
> To ease the steps and lift the load
> Of souls that falter on the road.
> He presses on before the race,
> And sings out of a silent place,
> And the dim path he breaks to-day
> Will some time be a trodden way."

Resolutely he has held himself true to this high ideal of his art, refining his gold and bringing to it every test, and few men of our day have more to tell us. Back of all the poetry of Markham lies a grand philosophy which sees that the great Soul of the World is just, and loving too. For him the import of life is deep, deeper than time and the grave, and an awful but judicial Spirit moves behind our human scene, weighing the stars, weighing the deeds of men. He is a hushed worshiper before that high benignant Spirit that goes untarrying to the reckoning hour, defeating the injustices of men. As we may read in the poem on Dreyfus:

> "O men that forge the fetter, it is vain;
> There is a Still Hand stronger than you chain.

'Tis no avail to bargain, sneer and nod,
And shrug the shoulder for reply to God."

From the mighty hand of God—so still, yet so sure—there is no escape, here or hereafter or anywhere. How compellingly, yet how compassionately, he teaches this truth in many a golden song. Since George Eliot there has arisen no more strenuous apostle of the human deed than Markham. Insistently, consistently, eloquently, he teaches the absolute justice that lies at the root of things, and the righteousness to which men must bow at last. Take, for example, his lines to "The Suicide." How few the words, how vast the significance! It is a whole philosophy with one dip of the pen:

"Toil-worn, and trusting Zeno's mad belief,
A' soul went wailing from the world of grief;
A wild hope led the way,
Then suddenly—dismay!
So the old load was there—
The duty, the despair!
Nothing had changed; still only one escape
From its old self into the angel shape."

No escape in life or death, save in obedience to the just and loving will of God. What is the will of God? What, indeed, as our own hearts tell us, but that we must be pure of heart and brotherly of spirit, making our daily bread "brother-bread," and living to serve our fellow souls? Markham has written of Religion as the Art of Life, and of poetry as the Soul of Religion—as witness his exquisite study of *The Poetry of Jesus*. But, profoundly religious as he is, religion means for him personal chastity and human ministry—brotherliness of spirit and deed. Therefore he bids us pray in words, but also, and still more, in works, for purity of soul, for loving fidelity to one another, for freedom and fellowship among men.

Like all the wise ones of old, our poet holds that we know as much as we do. Friar Hilary, in "The Hindered Quest," inured in his cell, sought peace in vain till, hearing a cry of human need, he went forth to do a kindly deed; then, as the Master told him—

> "You turned at last your rusty key
> And left the door ajar for Me,"—

which states in a thumbnail space enough for a creed and a dozen commentaries. So also in "The Angelus," that collect for any day in the week, and for every month in the year; and also in "The Father's Business," to name two of many poems. To the old, brutal question of Cain, "Am I my brother's keeper?" Markham makes reply that we are born for the practice of the Golden Rule, and our destiny is to learn to live and let live, to think and let think, building a social order that is wise and just and pure.

> "There is a destiny that makes us Brothers;
>   None goes his way alone;
>   All we send into the lives of others
>   Comes back into our own."

Indeed, our poet holds that the need of man may be summed up in Bread, Beauty, and Brotherhood—Bread, the symbol of physical necessities which must be met ere man can rise to the higher human life; Beauty, that manna from heaven to feed the hungry soul on its pilgrimage; and Brotherhood, the one prophetic word which describes the translation of the ideal into the real. When we learn to be brotherly, men will not be used to make money, but money will be used to make men. Aye, when we have mastered the fine art of freedom, justice and kindly living, the weary tragedy of human history will become a chant of victory. And until we learn the brotherly life "we men are slaves and travel downward to the dust of graves." Here is our material; here our tools and our divine design:

> "We men of earth have here the stuff
>   Of Paradise—we have enough!
>   We need no other thing to build
>   The stairs into the Unfulfilled—

> No other ivory for the doors—
> No other marble for the floors—
> No other cedar for the beam
> And dome of man's immortal dream.
> Here on the paths of every day—
> Here on the common human way—
> Is all the busy gods would take
> To build a heaven, to mold and make
> New Edens. Ours the stuff sublime
> To build Eternity in time."

America, in the vision of Markham, is the last great hope of man, because it offers an opportunity for the practice of Brotherhood. That is its imperious errand among the nations, and "The Need of the Hour," and all hours, is for fearless, faithful leadership of honest and true men "star-led to build the world again"—such leadership as we had when Lincoln lived. Surely Markham has written the noblest of all poems in praise of Lincoln. There is not another like it anywhere. If he had written nothing else, he would be entitled to our lasting and grateful remembrance. In a wild and fateful hour, when the nation was in dire plight, the Norn-Mother bent the heavens and came down to make a man to match the mortal need:

> "She took the tried clay from the common road—
> Clay warm yet with the genial heat of earth—
> Dashed through it all a strain of prophecy;
> Then mixed laughter with the serious stuff.

It was a stuff to wear for centuries,
A man that matched the mountains and compelled
The stars to look our way and honor us."

Truly he is a "good gray poet"—blessings on his head!—so gracious to know, so glorious to hear, simple, unaffected, kindly, athrob with faith and hope and love. His last book, *The Shoes of Happiness,* is in some ways his best. His message is the same as of yore, but it becomes richer, deeper and more varied in its exposition—sun-bright sonnets, deep-hearted lyrics coming to the aid of stories, parables and quatrains—and Longfellow might envy the exquisite grace of "The Jugglers of Touraine." The group of songs under "The Hero of the Cross," notable alike in insight and art, are reverent, austere, beautiful, and worthy of high rank in the Christian Melody. He is of those who know the way to Emmaus, and the White Comrade who journeys with us when we walk that sunset path. The first lines of this last book are familiar to my readers, but they are too characteristic of the inclusive fellowship of the man and the wise strategy of his love to omit:

"He drew a circle that shut me out—
Heretic, rebel, a thing to flout,
But love and I had the wit to win:
We drew a circle that took him in."

Apollo has been kind to our poet-friend and Brother, granting him in its fullness the prayer of Horace: a sane and healthy old age consoled by sweet song. His idealism has not waned with the years. Time has taught him a deeper faith that forereaches the greater to-morrow that he so surely sees is on the way. It may not come in perfectness in his day, or in ours, but come it will, as morning follows night:

> "Come, clear the way, then, clear the way;
> Blind creeds and kings have had their day.
> Break the dead branches from the path;
> Our hope is in the aftermath—
> Our hope is in heroic men,
> Star-led to build the world again.
> To this event the ages ran:
> Make way for Brotherhood—make way for Man!"

Chapter XVIII

ALBERT PIKE [1]

This is a great day in the history of Masonry, a way-mark in the midst of the years, at once a point whence to look back and a prophecy of times to come. To-day, far and near, men are gathered in the temples of our order to recall the name, and image, and labors of one of the noblest and most variously gifted men of this land, and by far the greatest Mason of any land. The lives of most men melt like snow-flakes into the past, not lost indeed but unremembered, as though they had never lived. But in each age a few names rise above the flood of years, linked with some high cause or some heroic and inspiring deed. Such is the name of Albert Pike, whose last wish was that upon his gravestone should be carved only his name, the date of his birth and death, and these words:

"He has lived.
The fruits of his labors live after him."

[1] Address at the celebration of the centennial of the birth of Albert Pike, by Iowa Consistory No. 2, Valley of Cedar Rapids, Dec. 29th, 1909, Charles Herbert Cogswell presiding. Mr. F. J. Lazell spoke of "Albert Pike, the Explorer and Journalist," and Mr. J. D. Stewart of "Albert Pike, the Citizen and Lawyer," the present address being the third in a series.

And to-day, if one were asked to point to the living works of Albert Pike, one might point to his poetry which still sings "Every Year," like "The Mocking Bird" in "Spring," or to his books full of lucid and luminous thoughts, as though some venerable and wise sage had returned from the world of ancient dream to write down his grave and simple wisdom. Or, if more is asked, we who stand in the temple of the Scottish Rite, remembering the legend on the tomb of Sir Christopher Wren, the designer of St. Paul's Cathedral, need only say to those who inquire: Look about you and behold the monument of Albert Pike, in a Rite which for the beauty of its ritual, the splendor of its drama, the profundity of its philosophy, and the nobility of its ethics, has none to surpass it, among the great fraternities of men.

To-night you have heard the story of Albert Pike—a sketch of his antecedents and early environments, whereby the man was made; his life as a traveler in far places, a poet of sweet melodies, a lawyer of learning and a citizen of renown; his prodigious industry and his versatile achievements. It is an inspiring record, in which all his fellow citizens, whether Masons or not, should have an honorable pride—a record which should set all thoughtful men thinking as to the investment of their own power of light and leading. But all this activity as poet, journalist, soldier, scholar, writer, orator, was only a small part of the labors of Albert Pike. Aside from all this, aside from even the chief work of his life, he merits honor as a philosopher, as a linguist, and as a master of simple, lucid and musical English prose. His mind, while at work here among us, was one of the richest, as his heart was one of the deepest, that was in communion, as a thinker, with his country and his age.

Genius, it has been said, is vast and varied capacity so condensed that it makes for itself a channel, as a river makes its way through difficult mountain passes, and then moves quietly amid scenes of peace and beauty to the Sea, which is its Eternity. Great in many ways—so many, in fact, that one wonders that he became proficient in any—it was as a Mason that Albert Pike was supreme, having few peers, if any, and none to outtop him. Into this channel he poured the bright stream of his genius, enriching the valleys with new loveliness, opening hitherto unknown seeds of thought, and causing faded symbolic flowers to bloom in beauty. It falls to my lot to portray Albert Pike as a Masonic scholar, philosopher and artist, in so far as this can be done before a mixed assembly. That, indeed, is a saving limitation, for he would be a daring man who should attempt in a brief time to review thirty years of the life of so tireless a scholar and writer.

Albert Pike was made a Master Mason in 1850, and from the very first the symbolism of the order fascinated him, equally as an artist and as a scholar. He was quick to see the beauties of Masonry, but no less quick to see the blemishes which disfigure it, and which have led so many to think its ceremonies trifling, its secrets mere pretense, and its titles and offices absurd. But he saw something else in Masonry, and it was that something else, along with its spirit of fraternity, that led him on. Everywhere he saw suggestions, dim intimations, half-revealed and half-concealed, of ideas which could not have had their origin among the ale-drinking, pipe-smoking craft-masons of old. So he set himself to study the origin of the order, his enthusiasm keeping pace with his curiosity, and when he found philosophers, statesmen, artists and jurists mingling with rude craft-workers in the early lodges, the hints of deeper meanings seemed justified. Not otherwise could he explain why such men left their clubs to sit in Masonic Lodges. At last he found, to his amazement and joy, that Masonry is the Ancient Greater Mysteries in disguise, Hermetic sages having poured their venerable and lofty teachings into its simple symbols—the teaching, that is, which Plato went to Egypt to study, into which Pythagoras was initiated; older than the oldest religion, held as a secret since the dawn of time, and imparted to only a few elect souls in each age. Here, as Pike saw, is the true antiquity of Masonry, and its chief claim to honor and respect—a sacred vessel holding in its symbols the oldest and highest wisdom of the race. If you would know the joy of Pike at this discovery, and the inspiration born of it, listen to these words:

"It began to shape itself to my intellectual vision into something more imposing and majestic, solemnly mysterious and grand, like those great rock-temples of India, in the glooms of whose recesses the mighty shapes of the grave, silent, serene, impassive illapidations of quiescent power and intellect seem to say, that, if they chose to speak, they could reveal all the awful secrets of the material and spiritual universe. It seemed to me like the Pyramids in their grandeur and loneliness, in whose yet undiscovered chambers may be hidden, for the enlightenment of the coming generations, the sacred books of the Egyptians, so long lost to the world; like the Sphinx, half buried in the sands of the desert. In its symbolism, which with its spirit of brotherhood is its essence, Free-Masonry is more ancient than any of the world's living religions. It has the symbols and doctrines of the old Aryan faith, which, far older than himself, Zarathustra inculcated; and it seemed to me a spectacle sublime, yet pitiful, that the ancient Faith of the kindred of our ancestors, a Faith already crowned with the hoar-frost of antiquity when the first stone of the first Pyramid was laid, holding out to the world its symbols once so eloquent, and mutely and in vain asking for an interpreter. And so I came at last to see clearly that the true greatness and majesty of Free-Masonry consist in its proprietorship of these and its other symbols; and that its symbolism is its soul."

And now, I trust, you begin to see, dimly, what Masonry is, and the motives by which Albert Pike was led to become its expounder. Here is the key to his life as a Mason and the secret of his long, unwearying labor in its temple. Here, also, was the basis of his belief that, by renewing the luster of those symbols of high and gentle wisdom—so high, in truth, that it must need be taught in symbols—Masonry could be intellectualized and made to appeal, not only as a liberalizing, humanizing educational force to all men, but also as a field in which the greatest thinkers may go in quest of wise and good and beautiful truth. Hence his honorable ambition to be the re-discoverer and interpreter of those symbols, and the expounder to the modern world of that fundamental moral and spiritual truth, that simple and wise faith which underlies all creeds over-arching all sects, which gave joy and hope to men before Solomon sat upon his throne or the Son of God lodged with the fishermen by the sea. It was an ambition worthy of any man and one which Albert Pike, by the rare quality of his genius, equally with the tastes, temper and habits of his mind, seemed born to fulfill.

All this beauty and promise, be it noted, Pike saw in the old Blue Lodge—he had not yet advanced to the higher degrees—and to the end of his life the Blue Lodge was the chief object of his solicitude and hope. Because there he found universal Masonry, all the higher degrees being, as he held, only so many variations, elaborations and improvisations upon the symbolic motif of the Blue Lodge, and intended to illumine and glorify its symbols. By every art of eloquence, in pages that march with foot-fall of great music, Pike sought to show men the hidden beauties of Masonry, begging them the while not to be content with trite explanations—given of old to simple workmen—but to go on and learn the precious truth the symbols of which are in their hands. It was a grief of his life that, owing to the apathy of men, and their seeming love of secrecy and show rather than reality, he was not able to do more for the Blue Lodge. He did not want to see Masonry lose its ancient prestige and become a mere social and faintly beneficial collection of clubs, and more than any other one man he has saved it from such an apostasy.

So far Pike had not so much as heard of the Scottish Rite. He seems not to have learned of it until 1853, and then, so he tells us, with much the same feeling with which a Puritan would hear of the ceremonies of the Moslem worship being performed in a Calvinistic Church. He imagined that it was not Masonry at all, but rank heresy, a sort of Masonic Socinianism, or perhaps Atheism; and he was sure that a Mason who devoted himself to it had deserted the flag. The cloud of prejudice—a result, perhaps of the rivalry of Rites, then quite bitter—hovered over him for some time. At length he saw that Masonry is one, while its Rites are many; and while he did not undervalue authenticity or accuracy, he did see, what so many Masons fail to see, that these things, proper in their place, are no more Masonry than red-tapeism is statesmanship; that it is the soul of the degrees that constitutes Masonry, the words being only the body, or shell. In this spirit he studied the Scottish Rite, its origin, history and teachings, and though he found its ritual in a crude and chaotic form, he saw at once the depth of its ethics and the beauty of its drama.

Our Scottish Rite appeared in this country in 1801, at Charleston, South Carolina, composed of the twenty-five degrees of the Rite of Perfection, with eight others added. It derived from a Supreme Council duly constituted in Berlin, in 1786, at which Frederick the Great is said to have presided. For its authority it had, in manuscript, a Grand Constitution, framed by the Prussian body—a document which Albert Pike afterwards defended so ably in his "Historical Inquiry," though near the end of his life he was led, by facts brought out by Gould, to modify his earlier position. Under this charter the Council announced its establishment to the world in 1802. It had no subordinate bodies at first, never many, in fact, until after 1855. This was but natural in a country, which, besides having a Masonry of its own, regarded the Rite as intrusive—just as Pike regarded it when he first heard of it. In 1814, it created the Supreme Council of the Northern Jurisdiction at New York, and the mother body took the title of the Southern Jurisdiction, reserving the territory south of the Ohio and west of the Mississippi River. Then came the anti-Masonic craze, which loomed into a political issue, defeating Henry Clay and almost sweeping both Councils out of existence. There followed a revival, and with it some friction as to the right to confer the first three degrees. But for the sake of harmony the Scottish Rite relinquished them to the York Rite,—as it is misleadingly called—though still claiming a legal right to confer them until years later, when Pike, after a study of the Constitutions, decided that he had no such right. So matters stood in 1857 when Albert Pike received the degrees of the Scottish Rite, to which he was to render such high service.

The following year, 1858, Pike delivered a lecture in New Orleans, by special request, before the Grand Lodge of Louisiana, his theme being "The Evil Consequences of Schisms and Disputes for Power in Masonry, and of Jealousy and Dissensions Between Masonic Rites." That lecture was—and still is—in my humble opinion, the greatest single Masonic address ever delivered, at once an analysis of the genius of Masonry, and a plea for that comity of Rites which now exists, and which Pike labored so zealously to promote. If you will look into that address carefully you will find, in seed, all the moral teaching that was afterwards to bloom so resplendently in *Morals and Dogma,*—the same calm and sure insight, the same scope and grasp of ideas, the same wealth of allusion, and the same remarkable mastery of language. The lecture was benign in spirit, nobly catholic in temper, and full of thought made impressive by the magic of art. It showed that the speaker had acquired a knowledge of the literatures and philosophies of the world, which was minute and extensive and completely at command, and that he had mastered by anticipation many problems which were later to shake the minds of reflecting men. He came forth as an inhabitant of a larger world, as one who moved familiarly through all the fields of thought, as one to whom the little jealousies of the moment were incredibly trifling.

Let us look further into that address, because it set forth not only his conception of Masonry, but his philosophy of life. His thesis was that Masonry is a benefit to mankind physically, morally, socially, and intellectually—physically, in that it seeks to better the human condition by establishing justice when it can, and by charity until justice comes; morally, by pledging men by solemn vows to obey the precepts of the great Teacher who preached the Sermon on the Mount; socially, because it pleads for liberty, equality and fraternity under just and merciful laws, made by all for the good of all; and intellectually, because it leads men to a large, calm, sane spiritual view of life—to faith, hope and pity. More than all else he emphasized the necessity to man of a hopeful confronting of the world as a moral and spiritual order. His lecture showed that he had gone to the central question of life—the difference between a materialistic and a spiritual reading of the meaning of the world, and that he had decided in behalf of faith in God, in the life to come, and in the final victory of good over evil. He did not simply say that these things are so; he gave reasons, and showed that this view of life is the corner stone of Masonry, the foundation of its strength, the beauty of its symbolism, and the secret of its gracious fellowship.

Masonry, as Albert Pike saw it, is ethics founded in faith and made impressive by symbols. Of no one age, it belongs to all time; of no one religion, it finds great truths in all. It is not a religion, but a Worship; and one in which all civilized men can unite; for it does not undertake to explain, or dogmatically to settle, those great mysteries that are above our human intellect. Beyond the facts of faith—the reality of God, the sovereign authority of the Moral Law, and the high Destiny of man in a life to come—it does not go. With the subtleties of philosophy concerning these truths, and the unworldly envies growing out of them, it has not to do. Masonry was not made to settle those; not made to divide men, but to unite them. It asks not for tolerance, but for fraternity, leaving each man free to fashion his own philosophy of ultimate truth. Thus Masonry is not speculative at all, but operative. It is the work of life, bringing the highest and largest wisdom to glorify the active duties of home, society, and State. This being no longer a precious secret among men, Masonry must walk in the open street, appear in the crowded square, and teach men by her deeds, her life more eloquent than any lips. Only by such practical moral art and social architecture can it retain its ancient prestige and justify itself to men.

Such was his vision of the spiritual morality of Masonry, uniting men upon those things which are the most important and the least open to debate, and thereby making for peace upon earth among men of good-will. This conception of the mission of Masonry Pike expounded, elaborately, in *Morals and Dogma,* briefly and vividly in his letter on "The Nine Great Truths of Masonry," but never more beautifully or persuasively than in a page-long essay, entitled "The Religious Influence of Masonry," published in Iowa City in 1858. Permit me to quote it:

"That enlightened Faith from which as from a living spring, flow sublime devotedness, the sentiment of fraternity, fruitful of good works, the spirit of kindness and gentle peace, sweet hopes, effectual consolations, and inflexible resolution to accomplish the most arduous and painful duties, Masonry has in all times religiously preserved. Ardently and perseveringly it has propagated it in all ages; and in our day more zealously than ever. Scarcely a Masonic discourse is pronounced, or Masonic lesson read, by the highest officer or the humblest lecturer, that does not demonstrate the necessity and advantages of this faith, and earnestly teach the two constitutive principles of religion—love of God and love of our neighbor. The sectarians of former days substituted intolerance for Charity, persecution for love, and did not love God because they hated their neighbor. 'Thou shalt love the Lord thy God with all thy heart, soul, strength and mind, and thy neighbor as thyself; this do and thou shalt live. Suffer little children to come unto me, for such is the kingdom of heaven, into which ye shall not enter except ye be converted and become as little children. He that loveth not his brother knoweth not God.' Such is the true religion; and that true religion is the very spirit of Masonry. Forming one great people over the whole globe, it preserves that religion, strengthens it, and extends it in its purity and simplicity."

One is not surprised to learn that Pike was made Grand Commander of the Scottish Rite the following year. He at once began to recast the Rite, taking away all tawdry titles and fictitious distinctions, rewriting the rituals, reshaping the degrees, some of which existed only in skeleton —others only in grip and pass-word—and clothing them in robes of beauty, grace and truth. To this task he brought all the resources of a scholar, the rare and vivid genius of a great artist, and a literary skill and charm which are the precious gifts of God to the poet-soul. He had built a stately home upon a hill overlooking Little Rock, where he kept his vast library and did his work. Then came the awful scene of civil war, and Masonry stood still. When the Union army attacked Little Rock, the Commanding officer, Thomas H. Benton—Grand Master of the Lodge of Iowa—posted Union troops to protect the home of Albert Pike in order to save his library. It was the mystic tie of Masonry spanning, like a rainbow bridge, the dark field of battle. But this act so enraged the rebels that when they returned to the city they immediately sacked the home and mutilated the library, for to such vandalism are men led by the wild passions of war.

After the war Masonry resumed its appropriate labors. Pike took up his task, revising his rituals, writing those noble lectures into which he gathered the winnowed wisdom of the race,—as though his mind were a great dome that caught echoes of the thoughts of a thousand thinkers: the dreams of Vedic poets, the meditations of men who lived on yonder side of the Pyramids, and the voices of sages long since fallen into dust. Then it was that he wrote high and tender prayers, and perfected, with such delicate art, those ancient dramas of the moral life, which, if a man once sees, he can never forget. Addison tells us, in the *Spectator,* of an author who wrote many pages to prove that generals could not have won fame and glory—"the sun that shines upon the dead,"—if they had not had men. Even so, on the other side, if men had not the leadership of genius they would only stumble forward, if they did not actually slip backward. And if, in 1871, the Scottish Rite was more widely diffused than any other rite of Masonry in the world, it was due, as all admitted, to the towering genius of Albert Pike.

And it was in that year, after years of high intellectual toil, that Pike published *Morals and Dogma,*—a monument of industry, scholarship, and genius. Time does not permit me to review that book here, except to say that there is no other like it for richness of thought, beauty and grace of style, and a certain large, gentle, far-seeing, finely-posed sagacity of simple moral and Masonic wisdom. Its first three lectures ought to be printed separately and presented to every man who enters the Blue Lodge. The further one goes into that book the richer it seems to be, as though one were climbing a tower and looking out upon an ever-widening horizon, until at length he attains to the sublime Doctrine of the Equilibrium—the poise of the soul between Wisdom and Power, Justice and Love, Necessity and Liberty, Self and Society, Reason and Faith; a mere shadow perhaps of the peace that passeth understanding, but at least a serene and balanced life far above the lazy, lingering mists in which so many wander. Apart from the main aim of the book, there is hardly a page on which one does not see the glint and sparkle of a gem, and it would be easy to make—as it is to be hoped that some one will make—"A Book of the Wisdom of Albert Pike," one page which might run as follows:

"Man is accountable for the uprightness of his doctrine, but not for the rightness of it.

"Influence of man over man is a law of nature, and the conquest of mind over mind is the only conquest worth while.

"Society hangs spiritually together, like the revolving spheres above. The free country in which intellect and genius rule will endure. Where they serve and other influences govern the national life is short.

"When the state begins to feed part of the people, it prepares all to be slaves.

"Select thinkers for legislators; avoid gabblers. Wisdom is rarely loquacious.

"Justice divorced from sympathy is selfish indifference, not in the least more laudable than misanthropic isolation.

"Deeds are greater than words. They have a life, mute, but undeniable; and they grow. They people the vacuity of Time, and make it green and worthy.

"The saddest of all sights upon this earth is that of a man lazy and luxurious, or hard and penurious, to whom want appeals in vain, and suffering cries in an unknown tongue.

"We must work because the capacity to work is given to us, and if no fruit of our work ever comes to us, so much the greater honor we are entitled to, if we work faithfully.

"Nothing is really small. Every bird that flies carries a thread of the infinite in its claws.

"Sorrow is the dog of that unknown shepherd who guides the flock of men.

"Life has its ills, but it is not all evil. If life is worthless, so also is immortality."

Here is the heavy ore of thought transmuted into shapes of beauty. Other Masonic writers are instructive and inspiring, but Pike always added the element of poetry that turned wisdom into art. It was so in life, more and more as the years passed, and towards the end, when life and love and sorrow had wrought their work in him, there was nothing in this land more beautiful than the soul of Albert Pike. It was like a temple at sunset, through whose stately windows the dying day pours its old-gold mellowness of light, touching familiar things as by magic into shapes rich and strange. Thus he was a Mason in the only true sense, a builder of a soul—that house not made with hands which in his faith was eternal.

It was a favorite idea with Pike—in private letters and public writings—that the Dead rule and the Living obey. What other men thought and said and did in the Past makes an iron network about us, and we cannot escape. If we try to annul a contract, the thoughts of the dead jurists of England, living when their ashes have long been cold, forbid us. If we would overreach a fellow man, the words of an old Roman lawyer, who died before Justinian, estop us. This act, Moses forbids; that, King Alfred. So, also, when we seek to bless our race by the gentle art of doing good, by deeds of daring excellence, we do but obey the injunctions of those great and simple men who lived here before us and left us their heavenly visions. Thus do we obey the dead; and thus shall the living, when we are dead, for weal or woe, obey us. By the same token, he argued, it is no misfortune to labor for the right in face of obloquy or apathy, for we thereby make it easier for the men of tomorrow to see the truth and do the right.

"And if the Soul sees, after death, what passes on this earth, and watches over the welfare of those it loves, then must its greatest happiness consist in seeing the current of its beneficent influences widening out from age to age, as rivulets widen into rivers, and aiding in shaping the destinies of individuals, families, States, the World; and its bitterest punishment, in seeing its evil influences causing mischief and misery, and cursing and afflicting men, long after the frame it dwelt in has become dust and both name and memory are forgotten."

By such large and prescient wisdom Albert Pike lived and labored, and it is therefore that he still lives, not only as a part of the great body of influence and law, as a spirit subtly coloring and giving beneficent tendency to this order, and through it to this age, but as a distinct and memorable figure whom we recall this night—tall, stately, with long white hair, his large brown eyes full of kindly light, his face blushing like a child's at merited praise—a vision of spiritual refinement and intellectual beauty. As he lived, he wrote and toiled and believed, and believing, so he died, feeling, as we feel, that there was that within him not born to die—as when, in the morning of life, touched by the wistful pathos of "Spring," he sang:

> "So I, who sing, shall die,
> Worn thin and pale, perhaps, by care and sorrow,
>   And fainting with soft, unconscious sigh,
> Bid unto this poor body, that I borrow,
>   A long good-bye—to-morrow
> To enjoy, I hope, eternal spring on high,
>   Beyond the sky."

Chapter XIX

RUDYARD KIPLING

It was at Bombay, "between the palms and the sea, where the world-end steamers meet," that Kipling was born, December, 1865. His father was an artist, his mother the daughter of a Wesleyan minister. He was named Rudyard, in memory of the pretty village and lake where his parents first met. After attending the military academy at Westward Ho, England, he became a reporter on the *Gazette* at Lahore. One day the Duke of Connaught asked him what he would like to do:

"I would like, Sir, to live with the army and write up Tommy Atkins," the lad replied.

The Duke gave him the right to go with the army, and it was thus that Kipling saw India, and what he saw he told in his tales. With opportunity came a mastery of the art of storytelling, and a style swift, vivid, and striking. Armed with his stories, he started for England, by way of Hongkong. In San Francisco, and later, in New York, he tried to find a publisher and failed. Disgusted, he set sail for England —having had a talk with Mark Twain betimes. In England his stories fell flat.

One evening Edmund Yates, editor of the London *World,* sat in his club wondering where he might find a story for his paper. He asked a friend at the next table to help him out:

"Why on earth don't you print an interview with Rudyard Kipling?" asked his friend.

"Who in thunder is Rudyard Kipling?" asked Yates, who had never heard the name before.

Having heard who Kipling was, Yates sent a reporter to interview him. That gave Kipling his chance. A born journalist, he gave such an interview as one seldom reads in a lifetime, and it set the town talking. Reading it, the editor of the London *Times* remembered a tiny book of stories on his desk which he had neglected. He reviewed it to the length of a column, and the fame of Kipling was made. Edition after edition of his stories sold. The seamy heroes of whom he wrote caught the popular imagination, aided by a style which reproduced vibrating air of India and the color of its life.

Since then most of us, at one time or another, have had an attack of Kiplingitis. At one time it was almost an epidemic, and if some of us have recovered, all retain a memory of its enchantment. His poems, with their sweep and swing, made men sing whether or no, and his stories carried tired folk to strange lands of fancy and adventure. If he is no longer on a pedestal, he at least has a niche of his own.

Kipling is a singer who does not need to soar. The charm of him is that he flies low enough to see the romance, the poetry, the mysticism of common things. Who else has written the pounding poetry of the steam engine—its glancing, glistening pistons, its great steel arms sending the ship scudding over the sea. A poet of energy he is, indeed, but he sees that energy is soul, is mind in action. Nor have we had another such personifier of things in literature. He makes the bolts and beams and screws of a ship talk. He reports the conversation of birds and beasts. He sings the song of the open road, of "the winds that tramp the world." He is a past grand pantheist.

So, naturally, he is dear to children, especially to boys, who live in the glow of the pantheism which has haunted man since ever he began to make gods in his own image. The *Jungle Books,* the *Just So Stories,* the unforgettable *Drums of Fore and Aft,* are immortal. It does not matter that the names are strange, and the scenery unfamiliar, for "in the hearts of children there is no East or West." Who can forget the story called "They," telling of the little lost children.

long since fallen into dust, who live in the House of God where the latches are low?

In such stories Kipling makes amends to woman for the awful things he has said about her. In his stories he laughs at woman, and in "The Vampire" calls her "a rag, a bone, and a hank of hair," a thing she can never forgive. But Jakin and Lew, Punch-baba and the Lashmar baby, wise with baby wisdom, and the pathos that clings to childlife everywhere, all must love. After all, Kipling has done no more than put sex in the background; and if he writes of rough men who do things, they are the men whom women love. Mulvaney, Ortheris, and Learoyd, despite their immense vulgarity, are real men, primitive, passionate, powerful—real men, no feverish, selfish clods of ailments and grievances.

Some one ought to make a Book of the Wisdom of Mulvaney, one page of which would be after this manner, with much more of a sort similar to follow:

"Hit a man and help a woman, and ye can't be far wrong anyways."

"Watch the hand; if she shuts her hand tight, thumb down over the knuckle, take your hat and go. But if the hand lies open—go on."

"Don't fight with ivry scut for the pure joy of fightin', but if ye do, knock the nose of him first and frequent."

"I kissed her on the tip of the nose and under the eye, and a girl that lets a kiss come tumblewise like that, has niver been kissed before."

"Whin liquor does not take hold, the soul of a man is rotten within him."

Under the touch of Kipling even slang takes fire and sings. He is master of sing-song and refrain, of melodies that trip and dance, and gaily or mournfully come and go to a banjo accompaniment. For vividness, for vitality, for the magic of the necessary word, there is not another like him. From the swinging ballads of the barrack room, he passed to the stately strains of "The Recessional," singing the Saga of the Anglo-Saxon round the world. Alas, he forgot in the fury of war-passion all which in that high song he prayed God to remember.

Kipling preaches a goodly gospel—good as far as it goes—albeit as far below the faith of Jesus as a banjo ditty is below the music of Beethoven. It is the gospel of men who live and love and do and dare, and feel the clutch of duty in hard places; the gospel of work and yet again work, and courage and loyalty through it all—with now and then a flash of laughter at the Fates who try to defeat man's unconquerable soul. His faith is that the Power that started the scheme of things going will bring it to an end for the best. The end may be Nirvana, he does not know. Nor does he ask. He leaves the end with Him who is the beginning—and therein he is wise:

> "It is enough that through Thy grace
> I saw naught common on Thy earth."

It is a religion of unchastened, faulty men—like Dick Heldar, McAndrew, Mulvaney, and the rest—who do their work, hold their peace, and have no fear to die. Its golden rule is,

> "Help me to need no aid from men,
> That I may aid such men as need."

More than any other great poet, except Robert Burns, Kipling has been a lover and singer of Freemasonry. He is the living Laureate of the Craft, crowned by divine right of genius, by his vision of the meaning of Masonry, no less than by the admiration of his Brethren. No one can read "The Mother Lodge," one of the noblest poems in the literature of the Craft, and not feel anew the ties by which a Mason is held to the old Lodge where he first saw the Light, and felt the consecration of a great Fellowship. It is instinct with the very genius of Masonry, the tenderness and tenacity of its associations. Masonic phrases and allusions—often almost too revealing—are found all through his poems and stories. There is "The Widow of Windsor," and such stories as "The Main Guard," the "Winged Hats," "Hal o' the Draft," "The City Calls," "On the Great Wall," many examples in *Kim,* whose passport everywhere in the army was that he was the son of a Mason—also in *Traffics and Discoveries,* and, of course, "The Man Who Would Be King," one of the great short stories of the world. There is no need to name "In the Interests of the Brethren," lately so widely read and so justly admired.

Still, if as a writer Kipling is a delight, as an influence he is, in some ways, a danger. Indeed, if we except two great human causes—humanity to animals and his fierce hatred of the rum devil—Kipling is hardly modern at all. He is an old Puritan who worships the God of battles. It is one thing to accept the hideous facts of war, and another thing to glorify them.

> "But for pleasure and profit together
> Allow me the hunting of man,"

is not modern in the true sense of the term, to say nothing of "On Greenhow Hill." For the typically modern movements—democracy, the advent of woman, the education of the masses, the dream of world-peace—Kipling has only a cynical contempt. In "The Sons of Martha" he actually saddles classism off on the Almighty, and even in "The Recessional" one suspects the snarls of the wolf of a narrow jingoism.

Nevertheless, so much of good as there is in Kipling—and it is much and very good—we keep among our precious possessions. He is a poet of labor and service, of virility and power. The poet of force is also the poet of force of character. He glories in a sound mind in a sound body. He holds that man was destined for good, and that he will attain it; he denies only the principle of absolute evil. He mocks at the thing which would appear to be what it is not. His protest is against pride, by which the angels fell. Surely there are no finer lines than those beginning:

> "The depth and dream of my desire,
> The bitter paths wherein I stray,
> Thou knowest who hast made the fire,
> Thou knowest who hast made the clay."

Long may he live to enchant us, this word-wizard, this magician with a wand of genius, this mystic of the barrack-room, this courageous, virile man who asks that—

> "Only the Master shall praise us,
> And only the Master shall blame;
> And each in his separate star
> Shall draw the thing as he sees it
> For the God of things as they are."

PART FOUR: *Prophecy*

Chapter XX

THE PATRIARCHS[1]

Surely the idea of such an evening as this was most happy. There is a day set apart in honor of our Mothers—God bless them!—and no one would detract one iota from its sanctity and beauty. But it has remained for this Lodge to dedicate a day to our Fathers, and especially to the fathers of Masonry into whose labors we have entered, and of whose prophetic sowing we are reaping the harvest. Of a truth, we honor ourselves when we meet and pay tribute to men who did so much to make Masonry what it is.

Some do not well know that there was a time, and not so long ago, when it was a courageous thing for a man to be a Mason. Prejudice against the Order was intense, often fanatical, and our gentle Craft was held by many to be a dangerous fraternity, as if its innocent secrets harbored dark designs. How different it is now.

---

[1] Address at banquet given by Crescent Lodge, No. 25, to Aged Masons, Cedar Rapids, Iowa, October 12th, 1914.

To-day our order is everywhere honored, and our gates are thronged with young men eager to enter its ancient fellowship. What has brought about this change of feeling and attitude toward Masonry? More than all else it is due to the quiet dignity of the men of the order, and the noble way in which they have shown what Masonry is in their lives. Nearly every man here, if asked directly, would admit that he was drawn to Masonry by the quality of its men. After all, the greatest influence of Masonry in the world is the silent, eloquent influence of character.

It may be interesting to some to know that such an evening as this recalls one of the oldest traditions of the order. If you will look into the *Old Charges*—the title deeds of Masonry, and a part of its earliest ritual—you will see that among the duties required of a young man entering the order was that he respect the aged. When, after a period of decline, the Grand Lodge of England was organized in 1717, who presided over the assembly? In the scanty records of that scene it is set down as significant that the Grand Lodge came to order with "the oldest Master Mason in the chair." Indeed, it seems clear that the impulse by which the scattered Masons of the time were drawn together into closer union came, as Anderson suggests, from "a few old brethren"; and during the critical period of transition, it was the old men who guided the Craft. For the first Grand Lodge, so far from being an innovation, was in fact a revival of the old quarterly Assembly, and was intended to preserve the ancient usages of the order. So that our meeting this night in honor of the veterans of the Craft has the sanction, not only of our own finer feeling for the fitness of things, but of the long tradition and custom of the order.

When is a man old? Age is said to be a matter of feeling, not of years, but old age seemed to come upon men earlier in former times than it does now. At the age of forty-nine Shakespeare sold his holdings in the London theaters, retired from active life, and went back to Stratford. Dr. Johnson felt himself old at forty, and Lincoln at the age of forty-eight spoke of himself as old and withered. The Roman senate was an assembly of old men, but there was a law that no senator over sixty should be called to his duties, lest his failing mind bring harm to the Republic. But it is different with us to-day. With us a man is intellectually in his prime at sixty, and many do their best work much later. Gladstone, at seventy, was just entering the second volume of his biography.

When is a man a patriarch? Let me tell you. Old age is that period when one sees the limit of life, whether it be at twenty, fifty, or eighty; when he sees clearly what once was covered by mists: a grave full of songs unsung, hopes unrealized, and ambitions unachieved. There are men, not yet thirty, who are asking the ultimate question: "What is the use?" These are the old men—old of heart, world-weary, smitten with palsy of soul, and gray with a sense of futility; these are the unburied dead. Think of a man asking such a question in a world where sunsets are like sacraments, and the hush and solemnity of the dawn is like the smile of God! Think of finding life flat, stale and unprofitable in a world where the incredible is an everyday fact, and the impossible is always coming true —a world where there is truth to seek, love to consecrate, and hope forever building its great Arch of Promise! Such a man has come too early to the sear and yellow leaf.

Also, there are men far along in years—walking down the western slope where the shadows lengthen towards evening—who are eager and alert of spirit, happy and forward-looking, their faith undimmed, their zest of life unabated. These are not old men. There is in them a foregleam of the immortal life. Years have piled up betimes, but they have kept their faith firm, their feelings buoyant, their sympathies active, and their interest in life fresh and vivid. How fine it is to see a man grow old reverently and beautifully, his heart aglow with the soft light of eventide and the glory of the star-crowned night! It is not strange that such men enjoy the authority of influence and counsel, of wisdom and prophecy, which Cicero held to be the trophies of age.

Each of the seven ages of man, as Shakespeare marked them, has its uses, its joys, its disadvantages, and its compensations. He is a wise man who takes life as it is, each degree as God confers it, each experience in its season—youth with its flaming visions, age with its serenity. For age is opportunity not less than youth, albeit in another form. Old age, to be sure, has its disadvantages and perils. Failing strength, stiff joints, "the lean and slippered pantaloons, sans teeth, sans eyes, sans taste"—these are familiar enough. Often it weakens the tenacity of memory, but if we can manage to forget what is not worth remembering, that might be enviable. With few exceptions—like Sophocles and Tennyson—age clips the wings of imagination; but it also cools our passion which befogs and perverts reason. Age is clarifying, and may attain, as Milton said, to "something of prophetic strain."

At least, it belongs to age, in a life well spent, to look upon the world with calm and wise vision. As Plato said in his *Republic* old age "certainly has a great sense of freedom and serenity"; but he added, "the cause is to be sought, not in the ages of men, but in their tempers and characters." That is to say, it is quality and not the quantity of life that counts for most. The fact that a man has lived on this earth three score years and ten does not mean, necessarily, that he is either good or wise. Some men are as foolish in age as they were in youth. Doubly foolish is he who, living to grow old, has not learned the priceless value of virtue and the wisdom of love. Time alone brings neither honor nor wisdom.

An eastern king offered a reward to the one who would tell him the saddest thing on earth. There were three competitors in the contest. One said it is unrequited love; another that it is the death of the young; and the third, who won the prize, that it is old age and poverty. I do not believe it, unless by poverty you mean that pitiful penury of soul which makes the gloaming of life so desolate. No; the saddest thing on this earth is old age and sin—an old man crass, crafty, hard, cynical, and impure! Great God! rather than come to such an end, let me die to-night, in the morning of life, my work hardly begun!

When we are young we draw checks on the Bank of the Future. Some men go on doing this, unable, it seems, to live year in and year out upon their current income. Not many of those checks are cashed at full value. There is nearly always a heavy discount, and more often they come back to us for lack of funds. When we are old we draw our checks on the Bank of the Past. Whether they are cashed or not depends on how thrifty we have been in laying up that treasure which neither moth nor rust can corrupt, nor thieves break through and steal. More precious than rubies is a wise faith purified by trial, a conscience void of offense, and the memory of years spent in purity, honor, and service. When a man comes to the end the only things he does not regret, and would not recall if he could, are the kind words spoken and the deeds done in love of God and his fellow men. At that hour an empty alabaster box, with which he has anointed some friend in need, counts for more than all the gold in all the hills!

Other things being equal, the advantages of age, though less obvious, far outweigh its handicaps. For one thing, age sees life in a long perspective and in a clearer, if dryer, light. It has a vision of the beauty and grace—and folly—of youth, which youth does not have. It is the young who despise youth and try to get away from it—the urchin longing to be a schoolboy, the freshman to be a senior. No man, when a boy, ever had half the joy running across the meadow as he gets from seeing his boy—not to say his grandson—on that very spot. It is the old who see the loveliness of youth, and love it. Youth is the drama, in which the actors are absorbed in their parts: age is the audience. By virtue of its detachment, age has a truer insight into life, and if it knows little of ecstasy it knows less of despair.

With the mellowing of life, there comes, also, a deeper sense of the kinship of things. Youth loves cliques, the more exclusive the better; it rarely gives love unless it is returned. Not so age, whose affections, if less turbulent, are less touched by selfish motives. Age makes little of human differences, and sets much store by the great common fellowship of humanity, seeing many ties of union where youth sees only discord. Work, too, takes on a new aspect with lengthening years. Old men do not feel, as young men often do, that the universe rests upon their shoulders. Nor do they imagine, as Hamlet did, that they were born to set the world right. They see that each must be content to do his little human part, and trust the fate of the world to a Power greater than man. If age limits a man, it the better sets his bounds within which he can work quietly and get something done before he dies.

Youth seeks very high for what age finds near by. It is when we grow older that the simple things of life begin to unfold their wonder and open long vistas of meditation. Nogi fought great battles on the plains of Manchuria, but towards the end he was wont to muse over an iris, finding in its beauty a mystery beyond his fathoming. Youth knows more than old age, because it knows so many things that are not so. After fifty our bottle of knowledge is so shaken that it is all of one color. When we are young we love Hamlet, with his obscure, haunting melancholy, but when age comes on we like best the wisdom of Prospero, who, by the aid of Ariel, won victory over Caliban. Age may not be more religious than youth, but it is religious in a different and deeper way. It thinks of God, not as a flaming fire, but as an abiding presence, made real by the revealings of the years —serene, infinitely patient, unutterably great and kind. Youth is for faith; old age for trust.

Why did Shakespeare all at once drop his task and go back to Stratford? No doubt many things blended in the making of the decision, one of which was that he was wise enough to know when to quit. Another fact may have been the elemental love of man for the earth, his great Mother, in whose bosom he sleeps at last. But perhaps the chief motive was a desire for quiet amid the scenes of his boyhood and time to gather the threads of his thought and weave them into a fabric of faith. There is a deep instinct which leads a man back to his native place, as many of you have made long journeys to Ohio, New York, or Maine just to see the sun come up over the hill or sea. One finds something homelike in his native landscape, and in the old haunts a man can fuse his latest thought with his earliest memory as he can hardly do anywhere else. Some such feeling must have led Shakespeare to leave London and go back to the winding Avon. And it was there that he wrote the gentlest of all his plays, *The Tempest*—a miracle of art, an allegory of the victory of man over fate and fortune by self-surrender to the highest laws of life.

Similarly, Albert Pike used to urge upon old men the study of Masonry, not only because it brings to us from afar the high and simple wisdom of humanity, but it offers to every man a great hope and consolation. At its altar a man may gather up his deepest thoughts which, in the busy mid-years of life, are too often left scattered in the disarray of a temple yet unbuilt, and fashion them into a House of Faith—a Home of the Soul. How to live is the one matter; and the oldest man in his ripe age has never found a wiser way than to build, year by year, on a foundation of faith in God and love of man, using the Square to test the rightness of our lives, the Plumbline to mark the rectitude of our acts, the Compasses to keep our passions within bounds, and the Rule to divide our days into labor, rest, and service. Love is ever the Builder, and whoso obeys its sweet law and builds after its pattern will not be left shelterless and alone.

After old age, what? Ever the evening shadows fall; ever there comes a time, to whomsoever is a man, when even the wisest knows not where he is; ever and ever the twilight—and after that the dark, when all the lights of philosophy go out, and only faith and hope and love remain. There is nothing for it but to walk calmly down the western slope, the sun shining in our faces, into the evening shadows—trusting the great God over all.

> "Grow old along with me!
> The best is yet to be,
> The last of life
> For which the first was made;
> Our times are in his hands
> Who sayeth, 'A whole I planned,
> Youth shows but half; trust God;
> See all, nor be afraid.'"

Bede the Venerable, in giving an account of the deliberations of the King of Northumberland and his counselors, as to whether they should allow the Christian missionaries to teach a new faith to the people, recites this eloquent incident. After much debate, a gray-haired chief stood up and spoke, recalling the feeling that came over him on seeing a little bird pass through, on fluttering wing, the warm bright hall of feasting, while the winter winds raged without. The moment of its flight was full of sweetness and light for the bird, but it was brief. Out of the darkness it flew, looked upon the gay scene, and vanished into the darkness, none knowing whence it came nor whither it went.

"Like this," said the veteran chief, "is human life. We come, our wisest men know not whence. We go, they cannot tell whither. Our flight is brief. Therefore, if there be any one that can teach us more about it—in God's name let us hear him!"

What has Masonry to teach us about immortality? Instead of making an argument, it presents a picture—the oldest, if not the greatest, drama in the world—the better to make men feel what no words can ever tell. It shows us the tragedy of life in its most dismal hour; the forces of evil, so cunning yet so stupid, tempting the soul to treachery—even to the ultimate degradation of saving life by giving up all that makes it worth our time to live. It shows us a noble and true man smitten, as Lincoln was, in the moment of his loftiest service to man. It is a picture so true to the bitter, old, and haggard reality of this dark world that it makes the soul stand still in dismay. Then, out of the shadow there rises, like a beautiful white star, that in man which is most akin to God—his love of truth, his loyalty to the ideal, his willingness to go down into the night of death, if only virtue may live and shine like a pulse of fire in the evening sky.

Here is the ultimate and final witness of the divinity and immortality of the soul—the heroic, death-defying moral valor of the human soul! No being capable of such a sublime sacrifice need fear death or the grave.

> "What has the soul to lose
> By worlds on worlds destroyed?"

It is the old, eternal paradox—he who gives his all for the sake of the truth shall find it all anew. And there Masonry rests the case, assured that since there is that in man which makes him hold to the moral ideal against the brute forces of the world; that which prompts him to pay the last full measure of devotion for the sanctity of his soul; the God who made him in His own image will not let him sleep in the dust! Higher vision it is not given us to see in the dim country of this world; deeper truth we do not need to know.

"There are more lives yet, there are more worlds
    waiting,
  For the way climbs up to the eldest sun,
  Where the white ones go to their mystic mating,
    And the holy will is done.

I shall find them there where our low life heightens—
  Where the door of the Wonder again unbars,
Where the old love rules and the old fire whitens,
    In the Stars behind the stars."

Chapter XXI

"SOLEMN STRIKES THE FUNERAL CHIME"

I

How many tender memories these old familiar words evoke in the mind of a Mason. Often in the open Lodge—alas, all too often beside the open grave—he has heard them march with slow, majestic step to the measure of the Pleyel Hymn. Never were words and melody more fitly blended, and they induce a mood pensive indeed, but not plaintive, rich in pathos without being poignant —a mood of sweet sadness caught at that point where it stops short of bitter, piercing grief. Yet few know when it was written and by whom, though many must have paused to muse over the faith of which it sings.

The hymn was written by David Vinton, a lecturer on Masonry and teacher of the ritual in the first quarter of the last century, whose field of labor was in the South, chiefly in North Carolina. Unfortunately, his path through life was dogged by the demon of drink, which left stains upon his character for which he was expelled by a Lodge in North Carolina. He died, so Mackey records, in Shakertown, Kentucky, in July, 1833, but Morris dates his death six years earlier and says that it occurred near Russellville, Ky. Morris adds this pathetic fact: "Nor were his own most beautiful words sung over his grave, on account of lapse from a life of sobriety."

In 1816 Vinton issued a volume entitled "The Masonic Minstrel, a Selection of Masonic, Sentimental, and Humorous Songs, Duets, Glees, Canons, Rounds and Canzonets, Respectfully Dedicated to the Most Ancient and Honorable Fraternity of Free and Accepted Masons," with an appendix containing a short historical sketch of Masonry and a list of all the Lodges in the United States. It was printed for the author by H. Mann and Company, Dedham, Mass., and more than twelve thousand copies were sold to the Craft. This volume contained his funeral dirge set to the melody of the Pleyel Hymn. As Mackey remarks, "This contribution should preserve the name of Vinton among the Craft, and in some measure atone for his faults, whatever they may have been."

From the preface of the Minstrel we learn that Vinton was appointed by Mount Vernon Lodge, in Providence, to procure a book of songs for use in the Lodge, and this suggested the book to his mind, the more so when he was unable to find any book to meet the need. This quaint volume, yellow with age, and alternating quickly from grave to gay, from lively to severe, tempts comment, did time permit; but our concern here is only with his dirge. Originally it had eight stanzas, only four of which are used in our ritual and burial service, and Vinton little thought that his lines would be sung for a decade, then laid aside, then taken up again and sung wherever a Brother Mason is laid to rest, "in the land called America."

II

Whether we hear this hymn in the tiled recesses of the Lodge, or on a green sward out under the sky, our hearts answer to its appeal. Albeit in less stately strain and more tender tone, it strikes the same note that sounds through the 90th Psalm—that mighty funeral hymn of the human race—with its chant of the swift death of mourning flowers, of the vanishing of man, and the hush of profound sleep to which all things mortal decline. How helpless man is, pursued by Time and overtaken by Death—his life a vapor that melts, his span of years a tale that is soon told. There is here that nameless sorrow, that unutterable sadness which lingers in all mortal music whatsoever, and will linger in it while yet we walk in the dim country of this world where Death seems to divide divinity with God. Evermore, in hours however trivial or tragic, in moods pensive or gay—

> "Solemn strikes the funeral chime,
> Notes of our departing time;
> As we journey here below,
> Through a pilgrimage of woe."

Touched by the twilights of time, the singer meditates and prays. He sees that the vast machinery of Nature carries forward the entire human race, and, without fail, drops them into one final sleep. Yet each departs alone—the father without the child, the wife without the husband, the judge without the court, the statesman unattended, the babe with no arm around it, aye, and king and peasant alike; and all walk one dark, inevitable path. In what silence and dignity they go, their faces all turned in one direction, following the footprints of a many-millioned multitude into the infinite. We who are compelled to watch their moving figures are powerless to detain them, and can only say farewell and then weep.

> "Mortals now indulge a tear,
> For mortality is here;

> See how wide her trophies wave,
> O'er the slumbers of the grave."

With all our philosophy and wit, death remains a bitter, old, and haggard fact which no man may either evade or avert. There is something appalling in the masterful negation and collapse of the body. It is profound. It is pathetic. Words are futile, and there is in that last silence what makes them seem foolish. What avails it what any man may have to say about death? The real question is, what are we to say to it, whether or not we shall let it have the last word.

> "Not all the preaching since Adam
> Has made Death other than Death."

Heart and flesh fail; and the generations come and go, following the forlorn march of dust. "Truly, as for man, his days are as grass; as a flower of the field, so he flourisheth; for the wind passeth over it, and it is gone."

III

Suddenly the shadow lifts, light shineth in darkness, and we see how true it is that the soul of man is the one unconquerable thing upon this earth. How wonderful is this ancient, high, heroic faith which refuses to admit that the grave is the gigantic coffin lid of a dull and mindless universe descending upon it at last. Life tries it, sorrow beshadows it, sin stains it, and yet it is victorious. When doubt deepens this faith becomes more profound, and out of the blackest tragedy it rises with a song of triumph. So it has been from the far time when the oldest book in the world was written, and so it will be until whatever is to be the end of things.

> "Here, another guest we bring;
> Seraphs of celestial wing,
> To our funeral altar come;
> Waft a friend and brother home."

Such faith is not a mere surrender; it is a force prophetic of its own fulfillment. At its touch the graveyard becomes a cemetery—that is, a sleeping chamber—and dark Death an All Man's Inn where a fellow pilgrim takes lodging for a night. Those whom we call the dead are the guests of God, whose love is the keeper of unknown revelations. Also, our singer sees that the social life of man, its warmth of sympathy, its sanctity of friendship, its dear love of man for his comrade, has enduring value. Because this is so; because life is brief at its longest, and broken at its best, it must be filled with Truth and Love; that so we may bring to the Gate in the Mist something too noble to die. Hence the wise prayer:

> "Lord of all below, above,
> Fill our souls with Truth and Love;
> As dissolves our Earthly Tie,
> Take us to Thy Lodge on High."

O Death, where is thy victory? Our trust is in God, that He who made us what we are will lead us to what we ought to be. Higher faith there is none. Even so, Masonry rests its hope upon the ultimate Reality, the first truth and the last, and it is therefore that its singer sees, amidst the fluctuating shadows of this twilight world, an august, incomprehensible destiny for man. As a song of triumph the four stanzas omitted from this historic hymn are worthy of remembrance:

> "For beyond the grave there lie
> Brighter mansions in the sky!
> Where, enthroned, the Deity
> Gives man immortality.
>
> There, enlarged, his soul will see
> What was veiled in mystery;
> Heavenly glories fill the place,
> Show his Maker face to face.
>
> God of life's eternal day!
> Guide us, lest from Thee we stray,

By a false, delusive light,
To the shades of endless night.

Calm, the good man meets his fate,
Guards celestial round him wait;
See! he bursts these mortal chains,
And o'er death the victory gains."

Chapter XXII

THOSE GONE BEFORE

Into the stillness of this hour, borne upon the wings of music and memory, come thoughts of those good men and true who walked "the broad, majestic days" with us, and vanished. To them, each and all—the young and the old, to those distinguished and those aspiring in obscurity, the veteran who died with long life and its rewards and the man whose face paled too early—the fraternal sentiment of this order makes recognition and speaks its tribute.

Their funerals are ended; their obsequies are performed. Words of faith and hope have been spoken by those whose ministry it is to comfort the sorrowing and to interpret the ways of God to man. They have gone to meet their destiny. But we pause here to remember them, as they would pause to remember us were they standing here and we sleeping out there "under the wide and starry sky." We seek to honor them, but it is they who honor us.

To have such men among us was a joy, and to remember them is a privilege. In their combined histories they were a power in the world; they filled many places; many were the lines of their activity; countless influences went out from their individual being. They added intellect and character to the communities in which they lived, and their going left the world poorer, all the more so for that to some of them night came in the morning. We would fain believe of men who lived so nobly, and so like a blessing to their fellows, that they are among the happy dead. At least, they know not the dreary, dull pain of waiting for those who return no more.

All sane minds, all high hearts, love life. We are not foolishly attached to this old earth; we are divinely bound. Many are the sweet entanglements, many are the ties that hold us here—ties of love, of friendship, of memory, of hope. Men do not willingly die; they are taken. A Hand is put forth from the Unseen and leads them away from the lovely scenes of the earthly life, with its color, its music and its charm—out into the vast Eternity. They follow a strange path of the soul, worn by the footsteps of a pilgrim multitude.

Death stops us. It stops our race. Men are engaged in their labor or about their play; they are in the city or in the field; they are at home or far away—and they are suddenly stopped. The shadow of God passes over them and they are gone. It was so with these men who were wont to gather here in other days. They had their plans and dreams; the tasks of life beckoned them; its warm loves held them—the birds were singing in their hearts. Whether in great or humble place, they had their prospects and pursuits, their ambitions and their hopes. All these are now come to an end. Their deeds are gathered in—a reckoning has been made.

What may be their resting place in the land whither they have gone we know not, neither can we imagine. Though they seemed to have melted into thin air, that is only seeming. They have not ceased to be, else life were a chaos of values and love and reason are set at naught. All those who were once here are still here: their words are they; their acts are they; and though these be forgotten, the spirit of their lives abides as a part of the great body of influence and law making for goodness and purity upon earth. Because they lived so nobly, it is easier for all men to see the truth and to do the right. If for no other reason, it is worth while to live well that those who follow us may live better.

The day is closing. To those who have fallen asleep we cry "Hail and farewell," and for each invoke the mercy of God! Peace be to them— they were our friends and we loved them! Gracious God, rest them—these men who walked with us here, to whom there was no place like home, and no music like the sweet voices of the fireside! Eternal life give unto them, O Lord, and if it be Thy will lead them through the gates into the city splendid—

"With light beyond the sun,
A land where dreams are ended.
And days and works are done."

Chapter XXIII

THE DAY OF ETERNAL HOPE

That a Day in Spring should be set apart to celebrate the ever-renewed evidence of the Life Everlasting is in accord with the fitness of things, as if the seasons of the soul were attuned to the seasons of the year. It is more than beautiful; it unites faith with life, linking the fresh buds of spring with the ancient hungers of the heart. It finds in nature, with its woven hymns of night and day, a ritual of faith and hope and prophecy.

So run the records of all time as far back as we can go into the dim past. Nor is it a mere fancy that has thus prompted man to greet the coming of spring with feast and festival, as symbolizing the victory of the soul over death. There is no death in nature; there is only living and living again. The earliest form of life is a tiny cell which does not die, but divides and multiplies life. When forms of life become more complex some cells become useless, and must be removed. Then death comes, not to hurt, but to clear away the rubbish, that the stream of life may flow on.

Indeed, death is the thing that makes for life all through the natural world. There would be no life, if there were no death, for death is the friend of life and supports it. We live to die and die to live, like all things else. Death is the miry road back to life again, and only by dying daily do we live at all. Nothing in nature dies or is lost, death being the dark room in which life changes its robes and marches on. Were it not for death, the stream of life would be clogged and stagnant, and there would be no advance. Such seems to be the meaning and ministry of death, and it is not only benign, but full of hope.

Easter adds a new note to the rhythm of life, confirming our faith and setting the world to song. There was no joy in the far-extending transmigration of the East where man, bound to the Wheel of Life, longed for death to free him from the weary round. The Greek faith began on a low level and climbed to a calm outlook, but it did not attain to joy. With them the future life was a dim, pale shadow of the life that now is, without its color or its gladness. Galilee is not far from Athens—only a short sail over a soft sea—yet, in atmosphere and appeal, what worlds away! Jesus did not argue about the future life. He made men aware of the soul and its august destiny. When he spoke life seemed to drop its veil and reveal its own eternal quality. With Him eternal life is here, as the sky begins at the top of the ground. He turned Hope into Happiness and filled the age-old faith of man with a new and compelling joy.

Such was the air of Easter morning, with its grace and joy and wonder, blowing through a world not hopeless but unhopeful. Men might deny the Easter story, but that morning breeze of joy they could neither define nor resist. No argument availed against it. Doubt was lifted and driven away like mist, and birds began to sing in hearts long weary and tuneless. It was infectious with the subtle, sweet grace of things sacramental, awakening faiths and hopes and longings long dead. It was a time when men— just plain men like ourselves—saw through the shadows into the life of things, and went singing through the world. Such was the fact, which even Gibbon records with wonder, and it changed the climate of the soul.

To-day, alas, the morning glory has faded into a rather colorless noonday, and one rarely meets a man of joyous and victorious hope. For the most part men to-day only balance probabilities, with alternating hopes and doubts, when they do not put the whole matter aside as beyond their ken. They are baffled, or else hoping against hope. Some hold their early faith to the end. Others lose it and never regain it. Still others believe, then doubt, and then believe again, for different and deeper reasons. So, at least, has been my experience in the few years of my life. Once heaven seemed near, as real as earth and sky. Then it withdrew into a dreamy distance, leaving this mortal life pent up in "the kingdoms of pity and death." After a time it returned, and to-day the eternal life is as real as the life I live from day to day. All the intellectual difficulties remain, but they have ceased to be doubts. Let me give some reasons, either one of which is ample to me, though not all of them together can tell the joy of my faith that "life is ever lord of death, and love can never lose its own."

Stand at night under a sky full of stars, and the awful vastness and depth of it will make you feel the appalling thing that makes men doubt the future of the soul. That still immensity strikes one dumb with a sense of the insignificance of mortal life. It is so frail, so fleeting, here to-day and to-morrow gone. Our faith and hopes and dreams seem to melt like a vapor into the void. Yet this tiny mind, hidden in the soft folds of the brain, makes a map of that sky, measures its distances, counts its stars and traces their orbits! Truly did Pascal say that if the heavens crush the soul it is yet greater than they, for it knows that it is crushed.

The Soul of Man, its doors thrown wide open by Shakespeare, its depths explored by Dante, its heights unveiled by Jesus—this alone were proof enough for me. To me the soul of a babe is greater than a star, and when one thinks of whence it came and its unknown wonderful powers, it requires no great effort to see, stretching far out over the Valley of Death, a great Arch of Promise. The shallow materialism which marked the last century is almost dead. Men are coming to feel the wonder of the human spirit, as they explore the uncharted regions of personality. Everywhere thinkers are asking the old question, "What is man?" and there is a deeper awe and reverence as they seek to unravel the intricacies of the mind.

One day, years ago, it was my duty to go and offer a prayer over the grave of a human wreck who had died by his own hand. Through the avenues of a great city of the dead we rode, four blue-coated policemen and myself, to the far corner where we laid our burden down with a prayer to One who knoweth all. Near by, in the weeds, one of the bluecoats found the grave of a baby and beckoned us to see it. The earth was still fresh over the little sleeper, and at the head of the grave the mother had set out a sprig of "Live-forever," like a sprig of Acacia. Those big burly men gathered about the tiny grave and looked down. No man uttered a word, but every eye was soft and dreamy when we turned away. Something had touched us deeply, something more than the pathos of a babe born in a city slum to sleep in the potter's field.

No logic, no learning, prompted that mother to plant a flower at the grave of her babe. Her act was as artless as it was lovely, done at the bidding of her heart, following the great intuition of her race that death is not the end of all. This is the account which life, untutored and unspoiled, has given of itself from the beginning—like the grave of a little girl in old Rome with her doll and playthings buried with her. For me that simple act meant more than the argument of Plato. All our arguments rest at last upon these profound intuitions of the soul; if they are invalid, we are only dreamers walking in a dream. Nor science nor philosophy has any other basis than is laid in the intuitions of the mind, which are the pledge alike of our sanity and our faith. That poor mother was wise beyond her knowing, and her simple faith has helped me more than all the philosophers!

In one of his sonnets Longfellow speaks of being at Newport News, after the Civil War, and while there he saw a nameless grave, over which was this inscription: "A Union Soldier, Mustered Out." That was all, and the poet added: "Here was a man who gave his all, his life, his name, that the Union might live." Aye, he gave all with no hope of gain for himself, at the behest of duty, for an ideal. This divine heroism of man, dying for an ideal and a future he will never see with earthly eyes, keeping his moral integrity at the cost of life—like the Master Builder—here is the prophecy of the eternal life. That in the human soul which faces death and defies it in behalf of truth and the ideal attests its own victory over death! It bespeaks a welcome home for all the brave, beautiful spirits who have ascended from the moral battlefields of time!

In August, 1917, on a day I can never forget while life lasts, I buried five hundred and twenty-seven boys. To-day, if I close my eyes, I can see those long rows of silent figures, each with a cloth laid over it, while I read the stately service of the English Church. They, too, gave all, even the blood in their young bodies, that liberty and mercy might not perish from the earth! If the universe is worthy of such servants, it will not let those boys die forever. It is unthinkable! To think so is to make life a horror and a chaos, in which Jesus and Judas are alike choked with dust, all moral values erased! In such a universe no sane man would want life at all, here or hereafter!

Here our gracious Freemasonry—so gentle and so wise—rests its faith; upon this basis it builds. Moral values are the most precious achievements of life, and they are not cast as rubbish in the void. The moral heroism of the Master Builder stands for us as proof of that in man imperishable and indestructible—the image of God in the soul of man—as eternal as the moral order to which it is faithful. Nothing can shatter such a faith. No acid, however corrosive, can touch it. Moral values are personal values, and if personality ends in death they end too. No, death does not divide Divinity with God. It is only the shadow of life! O my soul, remember and rejoice!

So, once again, borne on that tide of Eternity which men call Time, we come to the day of all the year the best—the Day of the Eternal Hope. Think as you will of the tragic and lovely figure of Jesus, this is His day, and all men must feel, if only for a brief time, the impress of His spirit as they read the story of His pilgrimage—His everlasting gentleness blending naturally with the soft-spoken Spring, when the finger of God is pointing the new birth of the world. Our little passions are as naught in face of that mighty Passion; our trials fade before that trial of Love